VILHELM HAMMERSHØI

VILHELM HAMMERSHØI: SILENCE

With essays by Felix Krämer and Florian Illies

Hauser & Wirth Publishers

Vilhelm Hammershøi: Silence

Felix Krämer

Danish painter Vilhelm Hammershøi (1864–1916) spoke very little. After visiting him at home in Copenhagen in 1900, German artist Emil Nolde later remarked, "he spoke slowly and softly. We all spoke quietly." He was "persistently taciturn," said his longtime friends. His lifestyle was so reclusive that they compared the painter with a hermit and sought medical explanations.

Hammershøi avoided social life. Art openings, theater premieres, and other public events were excruciating for him. This makes it hardly surprising that his biography was unspectacular. Born in 1864 in Copenhagen as the son of a merchant, he maintained an intimate connection to his hometown for his whole life. At an early age Hammershøi's mother recognized her second-eldest son's artistic talent, which would be cultivated with private drawing instruction from the age of eight. At only fifteen, he enrolled as a student at the Royal Danish Art Academy in Copenhagen. He continued his education at the School of Free Studies, founded a short time earlier by unsatisfied students in protest of the antiquated teaching methods at the Royal Academy. Peder Severin Krøyer, who was a famous international painter at the time, was one of his teachers there. Krøyer is reputed to have said that he did not understand his pupil but also did not want to influence him, because he was certain that Hammershøi would produce an extraordinary body of work.

Despite his reclusive nature, Hammershøi was involved in several Danish art scandals that catapulted him to fame. Although their reaction is difficult to understand from today's perspective, the academy professors and a sizable portion of the Danish public were incensed by his exhibition debut, *Portrait of Young Woman. The Artist's Sister, Anna Hammershøi* (fig. 1). With its muted colors, its nervous and slightly blurred brushwork, and its indefinite perspective construction, which makes it difficult for the viewer to take a fixed standpoint, the picture did not meet contemporary expectations of a painting. While he earned his classmates' admiration, the professors at the academy withheld their approval. In conservative Denmark, Hammershøi's pictures continued to elicit discussions in the following years as well.

Among Hammershøi's earliest paintings, the two small-format depictions of farm buildings from 1883 already display essential characteristics of his art. In *Landscape with a Barn*, the building obstructs the view of the landscape (p. 52). The building extends like a wall from one edge of the picture to the other. Apart for two treetops peeking out from behind the roof and a bit of greenery in the foreground, the work is devoid of nature. As so often in Hammershøi's pictures, the sky is gray, and neither wind nor birds animate the scene. The world appears silent and motionless. What appears at first glance as an unassuming scene confounds viewers with its radicality: in addition to the deliberate obstruction of view, the high degree of abstraction was highly unusual for the period.

The radical composition of the painting *Farmhouse* is also surprising (p. 53). It depicts a building whose roof and façade fill most of the pictorial field. It is unclear whether this shows a corner of the building or a flat façade: while the form of the roof along the upper edge of the painting includes a small sliver of sky that suggests there are two separate roofs, this impression is disrupted by the

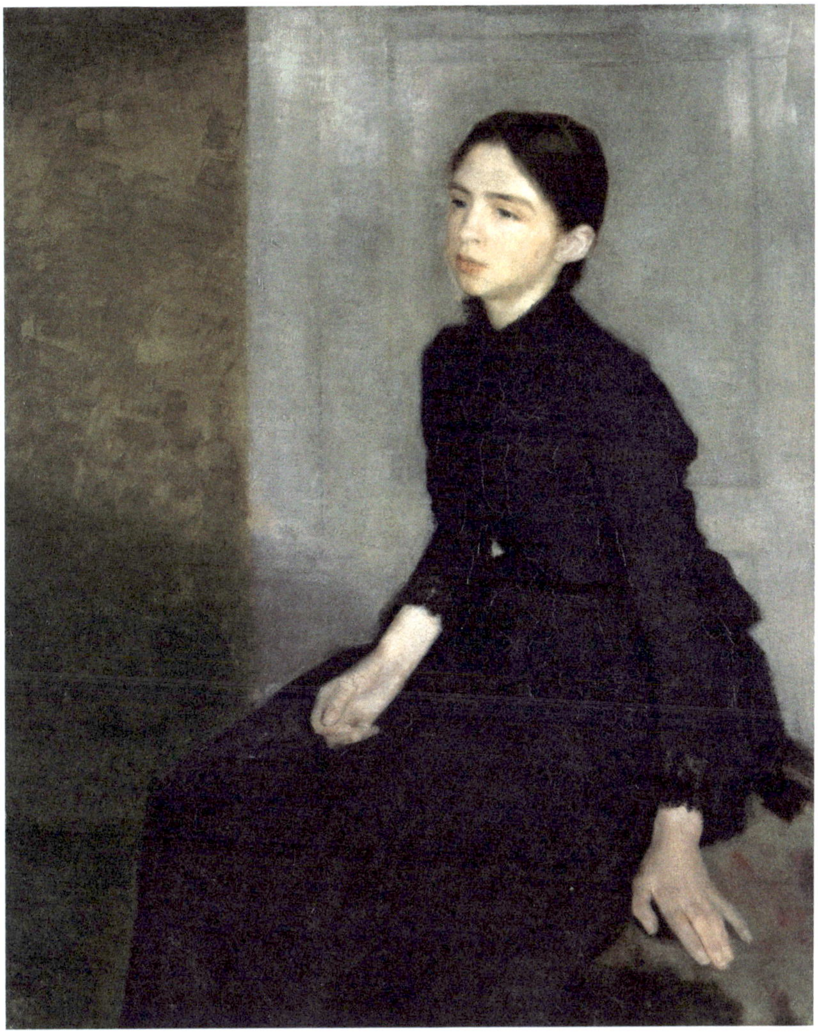

fig. 1

Vilhelm Hammershøi
Portrait of Young Woman. The Artist's Sister, Anna Hammershøi, 1885
Oil on canvas
44 1/8 × 36 inches (112 × 91.5 cm)
Hirschsprung Collection, Copenhagen

horizontally continuous roof edge and the perspective used in the depiction of the windows. In both works, Hammershøi plays with the expectations of the viewer who seeks clear answers. Like a reversible image, things remain in flux.

Another early work, *Interior with White Door and Yellow Wardrobe* (p. 49), also follows this approach. Created in 1886, this painting is Hammershøi's very first interior. It employs the essential characteristics of his artistic oeuvre, and once again, the rigid, graphic structure of the composition is unusual: the artist confronts the viewer head-on with a closed door. However, like the whole picture, the door is depicted so summarily that the door handle and frame are missing. It is mainly the proportions and the position on the wall that suggest a door. While the area of wall to its left is empty, to the right of the door stands a large wardrobe, upon which a light-colored bowl can be made out. The dimensions of the piece of furniture can only be guessed at; a shadow cloaks its contours in darkness, and it is also cut off by the edge of the picture. Exactly as in the farmstead pictures, Hammershøi omits any anecdotal detail in this interior. The motif, too, is utterly banal. There is nothing here that would be considered worthy of depiction according to a classical understanding of art; it is the way Hammershøi depicts it that makes it intriguing.

Although Hammershøi lived in seclusion in Copenhagen, he made frequent trips abroad to European capitals of the art world and was well informed about the art of his time. After his marriage to Ida Ilsted, the sister of his fellow student Peter Ilsted, the artist spent half a year in Paris in 1891. More important for him than the developments of contemporary art, however, was seventeenth-century Dutch genre painting; he had previously admired such works in Holland and Belgium. Alongside Jan Vermeer's mysterious interiors, he was

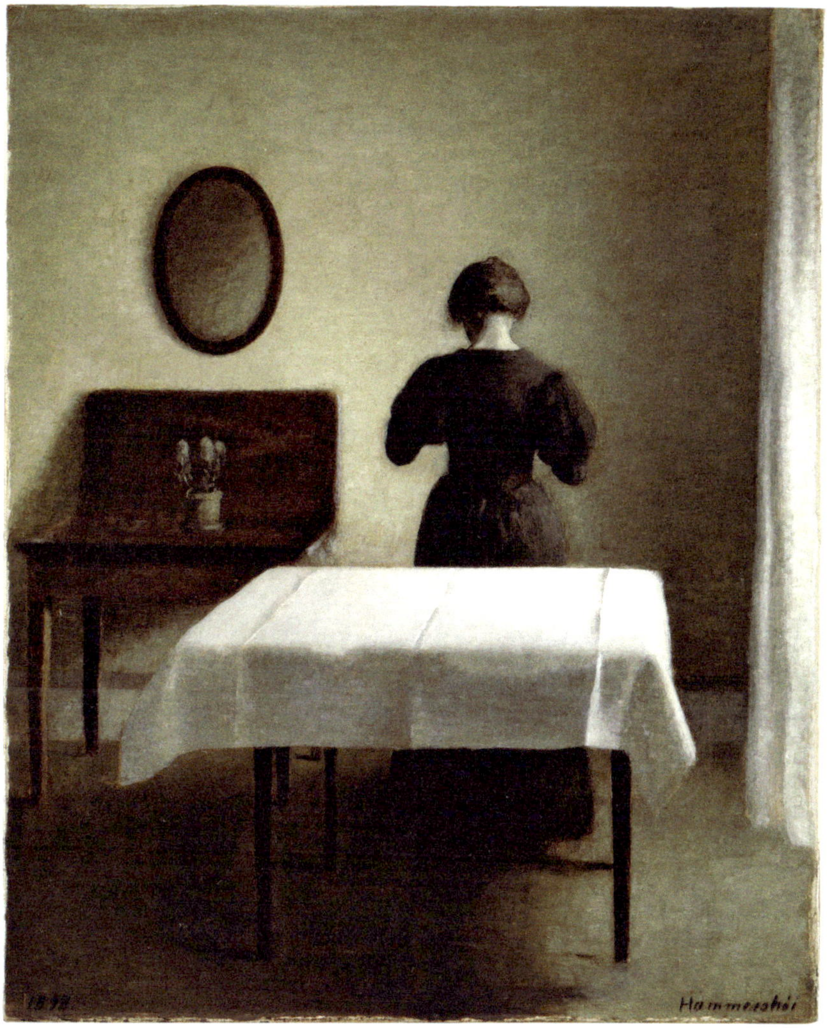

fig. 2

Vilhelm Hammershøi
Interior, 1898
Oil on canvas
20 1/4 × 18 1/8 inches (51.5 × 46 cm)
Nationalmuseum Stockholm

fascinated by the domestic scenes of Pieter de Hooch, Emanuel Witte, and Pieter Janssens Elinga. Hammershøi was by no means alone: these pictures enjoyed great popularity among art connoisseurs of the time and were interpreted as both reflections of a well-ordered quotidian life and visions of private happiness.

London played an important role for Hammershøi, who visited the city five times. Apart from his hometown, he spent no greater amount of time anywhere else. It was here that the artist painted *Interior with a Standing Woman* (p. 55) in 1898. The picture is closely related to another painting produced simultaneously, which is now part of the collection of the Nationalmuseum in Stockholm (fig. 2). While this work shows Ida standing behind a table covered with a white cloth, the piece of furniture is absent in the second version. Here, Ida stands in an open space, her back turned to the viewer once again. In each picture a half-folded table has been placed against the wall and an oval mirror hangs above it. Although

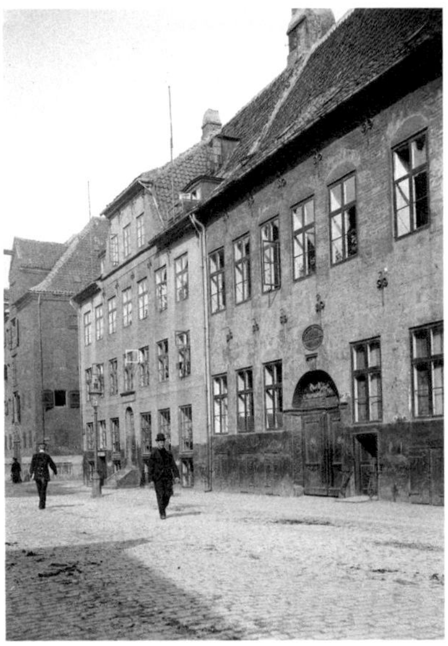

fig. 3

Strandgade 30–32, 1903

the viewer looks head-on into the mirror, no reflection can be seen in it; only a gray surface can be made out. In the Stockholm version, the painter placed a potted plant on the folding table; in the other picture, he added an empty white candle holder. It is not clear whether Ida is reading a newspaper or holding a white tablecloth in her hand.

Although Hammershøi is known primarily for depictions of interiors such as this one, until his return from London the genres of portrait, landscape, and architectural scene stood on equal footing in his oeuvre. This changed only after he moved to Strandgade 30 immediately following his return to Copenhagen. The seventeenth-century brick building in the Christianshavn district, where the artist lived from 1898 to 1909, still stands (figs. 3, 4), along with the interior courtyard with its many windows, which he painted in ca. 1905 (p. 69). The apartment on the second floor was not only his home and studio; it also became his most important motif. The rooms contained

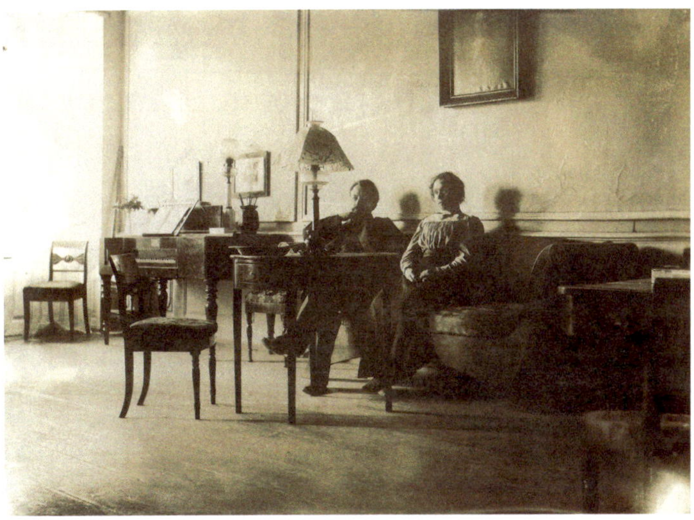

fig. 4

Vilhelm and Ida Hammershøi in the living room of Strandgade 30, ca. 1905

a small number of historical furnishings and objects, which appear repeatedly in Hammershøi's pictures. Neither the sparse furniture nor the simplicity of the household objects is representative of contemporary taste, which preferred richly decorated and opulently furnished spaces.

Four pictures painted between 1900 and 1906 are exemplary of the interior depictions that Hammershøi produced at Strandgade 30. The two earliest works, both created two years after they moved in, show Ida in the rooms facing the street. While the painting *Interior with Woman Placing Branches in Vase on Table* (p. 58) is unusually accessible for the artist's oeuvre, since we not only see Ida from the front but also can clearly make out what she is doing, *Interior with a Writing Desk* (p. 61) accords with his preference to leave viewers in uncertainty. It depicts Ida standing at a window and half concealed by a bookcase. Presumably she is reading a letter in the light coming through the window, but neither the contents of the missive nor her reaction to it can be inferred. A massive writing desk claims most of the space within the picture's composition: it is slightly offset from the center axis, positioned frontally before the wall. A small vase standing on the desk and three pictures hanging on the wall draw the gaze to it even more. Ida is strikingly small in relation to the furniture, which in turn appears even more substantial. The distribution of the objects in space is also unsettling: while the right side of the picture remains empty, all the named elements of the depiction are found on the left side. This creates a tension that inflects the initially so harmonious-seeming composition. With these compositional decisions, Hammershøi undermines the conventional hierarchy: contrary to our expectations, it is not Ida that commands the scene but, rather, the writing desk.

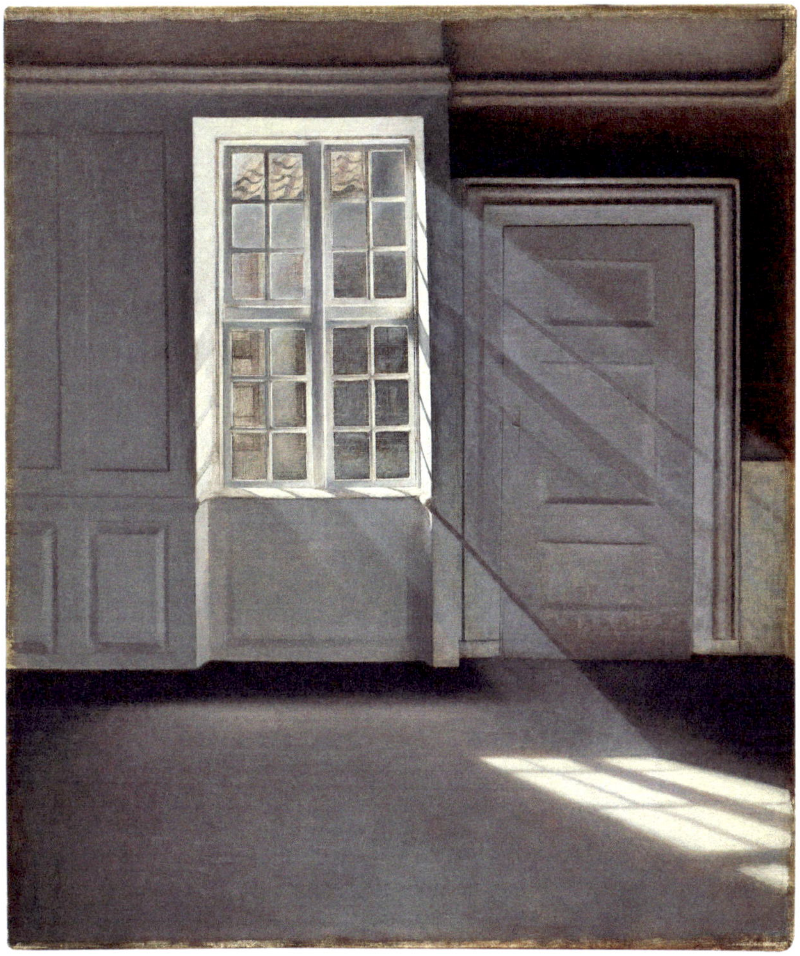

fig. 5

Vilhelm Hammershøi
Sunbeams or Sunlight. Dust Motes Dancing in the Sunbeams. Strandgade 30, 1900
Oil on canvas
27 ½ × 23 ¼ inches (70 × 59 cm)
Ordrupgaard, Copenhagen

Numerous interiors—such as the work *Interior with the Artist's Wife, Seen from Behind* (p. 71) painted in 1901—show Ida from behind wearing a dark, floor-length dress. She stands next to a piano, her arms folded, her head slightly bowed. Again, what Ida is doing remains unclear. A white chair is positioned at the piano; behind it on the instrument is an open music book. Two pictures hang on the wall; the white mat suggests they are prints. The motifs cannot be discerned. All the objects represented here are familiar from the Hammershøi cosmos and appear in many of his pictures. Even if the artist always painted objects that really existed, it would be naive to think that he constantly rearranged and reconfigured the apartment.

Woman before a Mirror of 1906 (p. 65), which was also produced at Strandgade 30, is one of Hammershøi's most unusual works. While the two interiors just mentioned show the living room facing the street, this view shows one of the rear rooms oriented to the courtyard. It depicts the window that is familiar to us from *Sunbeams or Sunlight. Dust Motes Dancing in the Sunbeams. Strandgade 30* (1900)—probably Hammershøi's most popular painting (fig. 5). Ida, at far left in the picture, seems to be in the act of adjusting her hair in a small mirror standing on a dresser. She stands turned slightly sideways and appears less static than usual. Because of the raised arm, her face again cannot be seen. In the left foreground a chair is positioned at the picture's edge, as if an invisible viewer who surveys the scene were present. As in no other picture by Hammershøi, the sunlight streaming through the window, the movement, and the space come together in a complex, tightly woven whole.

Even after moving out of Strandgade 30—the building was then in such dilapidated condition that it threatened to collapse—Hammershøi continued to paint the private spaces of his apartments. In

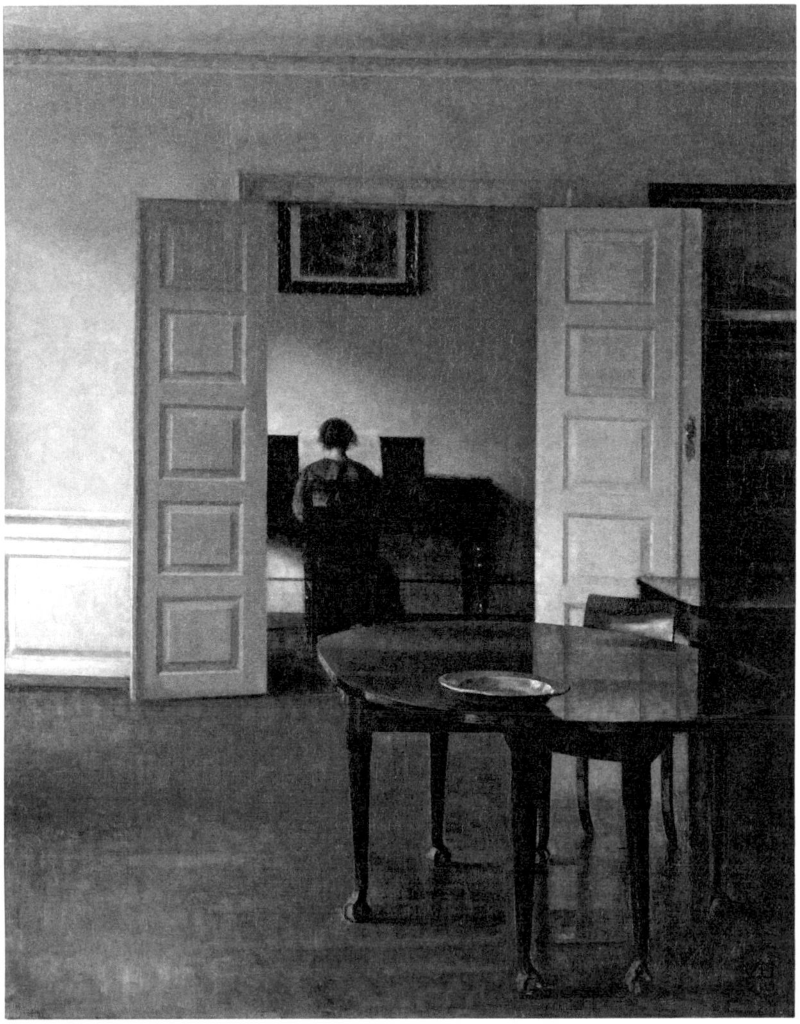

fig. 6

Vilhelm Hammershøi
Interieur with Ida Playing the Piano, 1910
Oil on canvas
29 7/8 × 24 1/4 inches (76 × 61.5 cm)
National Museum of Western Art, Tokyo

addition to paintings, he also produced several drawings. *Sunlit Interior* (1910; p. 23) is the drawn version of a painting from 1910 (fig. 6). It cannot be said with certainty which of the two works was created first. The works show the spacious living and music room of the apartment at Bredgade 25, where the artist lived for three years starting in 1910. During this period, Hammershøi also painted a self-portrait showing himself with his wife (pp. 82–83). While the artist stands at the easel and looks directly at the viewer, Ida remains in the background, depicted from behind in a white dress. The entire interior is enclosed by an elliptical frame form, which makes clear that the world of the artist and that of the viewer are two separate spheres.

Among Hammershøi's most uncompromising works are the *Interior of the Great Hall in Lindegaarden* of 1909 (pp. 72–73) and *Interior in London, Brunswick Square*, which he painted in 1912 during his last visit to England (pp. 62–63). Both pictures confront the viewer with prospects of vacant rooms: the painting created in 1909 depicts, as if seen through a wide-angle lens, a large, empty ballroom whose playfully decorative wall and ceiling panels evidently captivated the painter. In the second work, painted three years later, the painter shows the view out the front windows of his London apartment. Contrary to what we expect from the motif of a window depiction, Hammershøi does not really allow the viewer to share the view outside. A street, buildings, and a few trees with sparse foliage are only schematically revealed in the fog. The importance of this painting to the artist can be inferred from photographs of his Copenhagen apartment: it hung in his bedroom.

Hammershøi's interiors are genre paintings that lack narrative and do not betray anything about the inhabitants. Although the artist repeatedly invites the viewer to visit him at home, he does not share anything private. It is an immense silence that dominates Hammershøi's rooms and whose presence captivates the viewer. This effect is strengthened by the palette, concentrated in a few muted colors, which offers no distraction. The artist summarized the unique effect of his colors in one of his rare interviews in 1907: "They can perhaps be best described as neutral and reduced colors. I am deeply convinced that a picture has the best effect in terms of color, the fewer colors it has." His paintings are composed of multiple layers of color. The artist usually worked on one picture for a long time, producing the nuances of the individual effects of color and shadow during the painting process. Working with nearly dried-out oils, he used short, broad brushstrokes to apply the paint to the canvas. His painting *Morning Toilette* of 1914 (p. 77) allows this process to be reconstructed. The rough and open execution of the painting, which exists in a second version, recall his nudes from several years before (fig. 7), in which the artist made his wife's face unrecognizable through overpainting. Here as well, this erasure of the face generates a feeling of distance that stands in notable contradiction to the motif.

Similarly, Hammershøi's cityscapes hardly correspond to the contemporary practice of depicting the city as a lively place of constant movement. His urban scenes seem remarkably lifeless and distanced. One searches in vain for signs of urban vitality such as pedestrians, vehicles, drying laundry, and smoking chimneys. This is also the case for the pictures that show the center of his hometown, Copenhagen. Even his contemporaries were reminded of abandoned cities because of the emptiness and melancholic mood of these pictures.

The painting *Christiansborg*, which Hammershøi painted in 1914, two years before his death, making it one of his last pictures, is exemplary of these works (p. 74). It belongs among a group of paintings

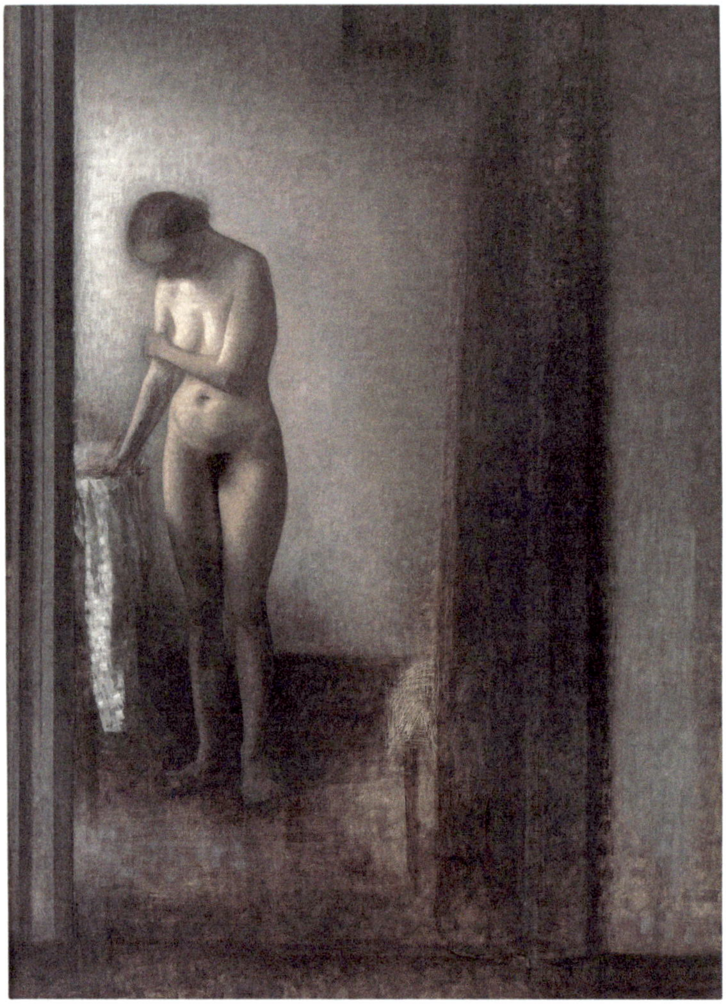

fig. 7

Vilhelm Hammershøi
Standing Female Nude, 1909–10
Oil on canvas
80 ¾ × 60 ¼ inches (205 × 153 cm)
Statens Museum for Kunst, Copenhagen

depicting the palace, located in the heart of Copenhagen, from different perspectives. The artist painted the building repeatedly at irregular intervals starting in 1890. In the pictures, it is impossible to detect that the main building of the palace had been gutted by fire, making this a construction site. Contemporary viewers were well aware of the building's tragic history and the fact that its reconstruction had been long and controversially discussed—the remaining work would not be concluded until 1937. In the painting from 1914, Hammershøi focuses on the buildings enclosing the courtyard and the Marble Bridge leading over the Frederiksholms Canal. From the low viewpoint, nothing can be seen of the palace's newly constructed main building. The perspective also makes the architecture appear more forbidding and closed off. The same can be said for the water in the canal: it is hard to imagine that any life could exist here.

This atmosphere of the uninhabitable also applies to Hammershøi's landscapes. Although he always painted well-accessible areas, he did not depict people or animals. In *Landscape, Gentofte* of 1903, a well-traveled tree-lined road and farmstead outside of Copenhagen can be seen (fig. 8). The noteworthy aspect of the depiction, however, is the dominance of the sky and the area of water in the foreground—between which a narrow strip of landscape has been slid. Here as well, it is evident that the artist, unlike many of his contemporaries, does not imply a Romantic longing for undisturbed nature. Rather, Hammershøi is fascinated by the graphic structure of the motif. The artist opposes the idea of an unbridled nature through the rigor of his composition and the austerity of his painting.

As is often the case, contemporary reviews contribute to a better understanding of Hammershøi's art. Around 1900, critics compared him with artists as diverse as James McNeill Whistler, Edvard Munch,

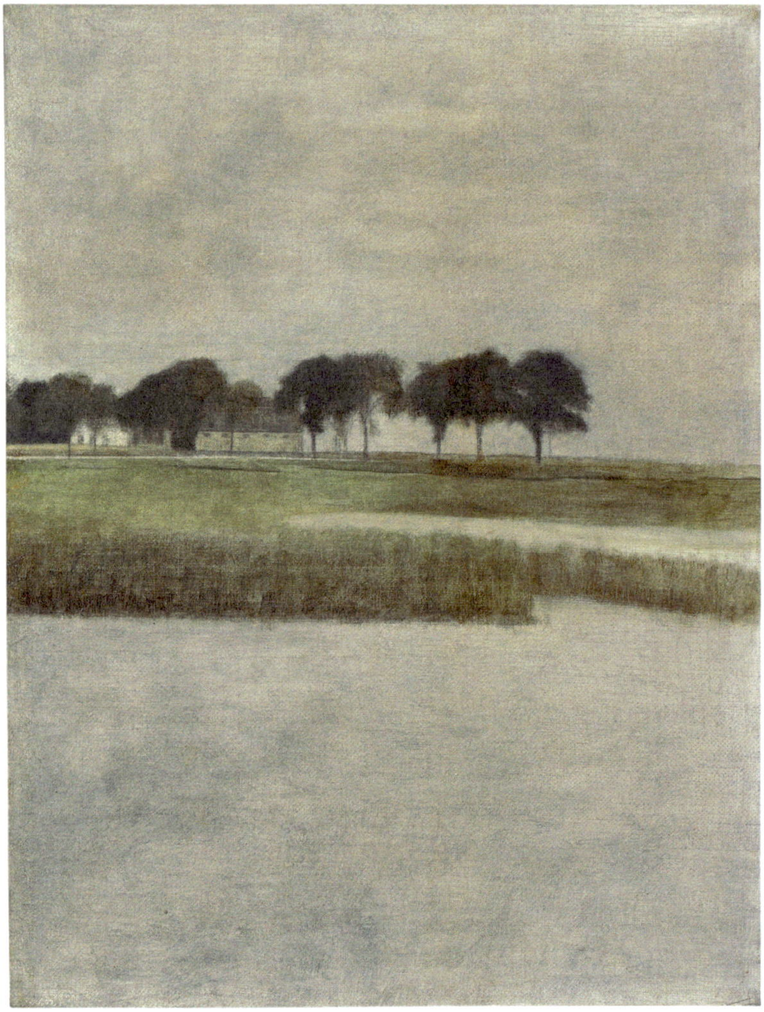

fig. 8

Vilhelm Hammershøi
Landscape, Gentofte, 1903
Oil on canvas
13 3/8 × 10 1/4 inches (34 × 26 cm)
Private collection

and Max Klinger: although these painters have very different oeuvres, their work was regarded, along with Hammershøi's, as a contribution to Symbolism. The movement is reflected not by a shared stylistic manner but, rather, by a related intellectual attitude of the artists, who believed they could recognize the essence of life behind the visible surface. Moreover, Hammershøi's painting was repeatedly associated with the works of Symbolist writers Maurice Maeterlinck and Georges Rodenbach, who sought inner fulfillment in silence and seclusion. Writing in his essay *Silence*, "It is only when life is sluggish within us that we speak . . . and no sooner do we speak than something warns us that the divine gates are closing," Maeterlinck stylizes speechlessness as an ideal form of human communication that leads to fundamental insights.

It is certainly no coincidence with regard to Hammershøi that Danish philosopher Søren Kierkegaard in the mid-nineteenth century regarded silence as the ideal condition for the search for authenticity and deeper knowledge. In his lifetime, the philosopher was admired as one of Denmark's most important thinkers. Hammershøi, who possessed an extensive library, owned seven books by Kierkegaard, including several first editions. Kierkegaard's most famous work, *Either/Or* (1843), was also among them.

Although Hammershøi's painting was also internationally received even at the beginning of his career, after his death in 1916 it was increasingly forgotten. His silent, puritanical painting contrasted too starkly with the restless experiments of the postwar avant-garde. Only the rediscovery of Symbolism since the 1970s and the related reassessment of figurative painting as an important contribution to contemporary art brought Hammershøi's mysteriously melancholic pictures into focus. While the artist was viewed by many in his time as an eccentric oddball, he is today admired as a kindred soul of Jan Vermeer and Edward Hopper. No other artist of the late nineteenth century has been granted such a rapid ascent in recent decades, from a painter's painter to a celebrity. Notable retrospectives in Paris, New York, London, and Tokyo have brought the unique fascination of his art before the eyes of a large audience. Unlike only a few years ago, Hammershøi is now prominently represented in the most important museum collections, also outside of Scandinavia. His work is also a source of excitement for many contemporary artists, as the exhibition *There I Belong: Hammershøi by Elmgreen and Dragset* at the Statens Museums for Kunst in Copenhagen in 2019 attests. The show, curated by Michael Elmgreen and Ingar Dragset, juxtaposed Hammershøi's interiors with works of the two artist/curators and works of many of their colleagues, including Monica Bonvicini, Ugo Rondinone, and Thomas Ruff. It is evident that with his paintings, Hammershøi strikes the nerve of today's generations. His art appears as a countermodel to the loud and hectic world in which we live. To pause, not to speak, to allow silence: this longing for peace and deceleration experiences its artistic form through Hammershøi's painting.

Vilhelm Hammershøi
Sunlit Interior, 1910
Pencil on paper
15 × 12 inches (38 × 30.5 cm)
Private collection

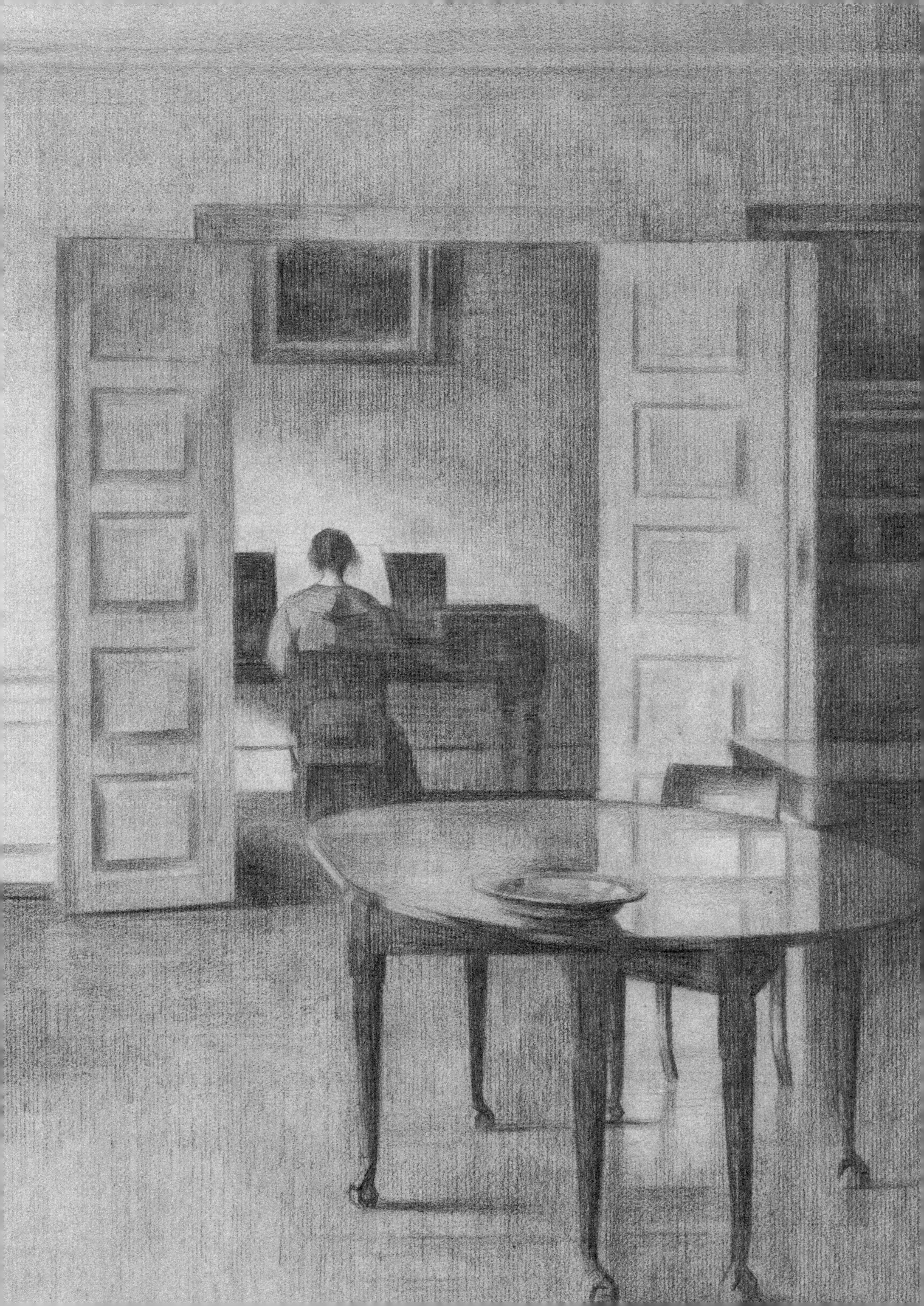

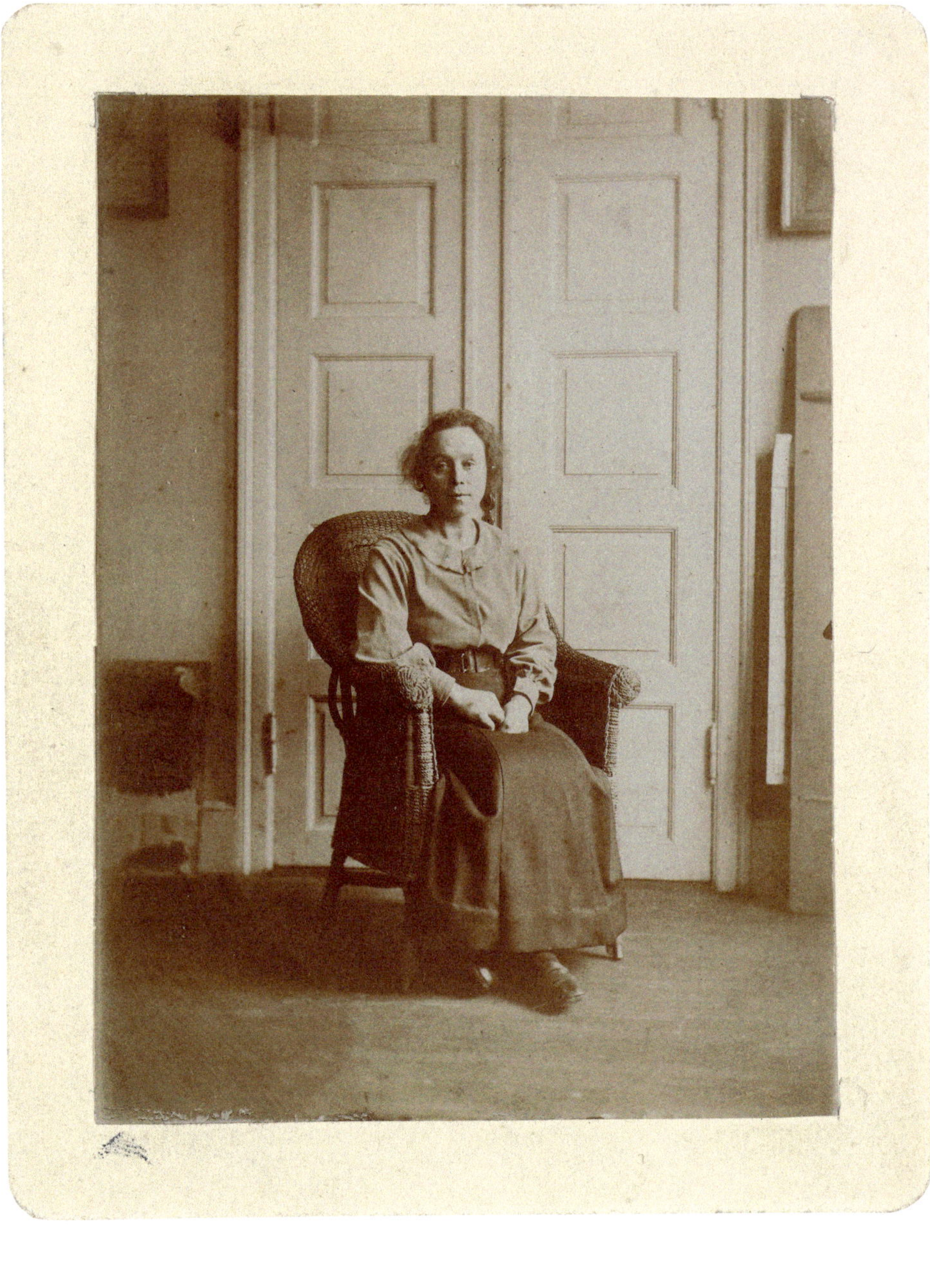

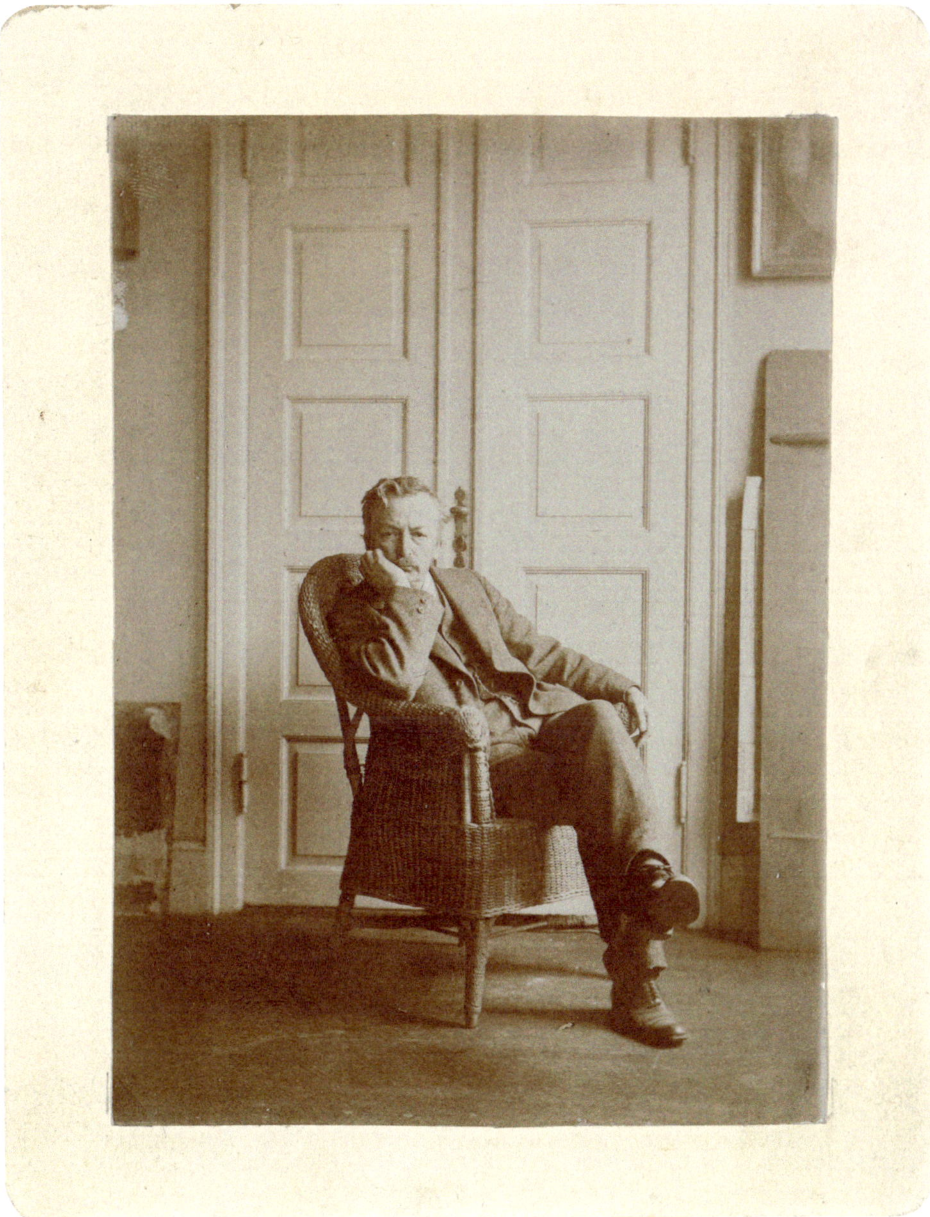

Ida and Vilhelm Hammershøi
in their apartment at Bredgade 25
ca. 1912

Florian Illies

Memories of the Future

In the Works of Vilhelm Hammershøi, Time and Eternity Touch

What makes Vilhelm Hammershøi such an eminently contemporary artist? He was only a visitor in his own era at the turn of the century: like an ambassador from the future, he always recorded the present as a time that had already passed. His pictures seem to be informed by experiences of modernism, that is, developments of the twentieth and twenty-first centuries, to which they could hardly have been exposed. Precisely this secret knowledge from a time that would not begin until long after Hammershøi's death makes his oeuvre into a much-needed component of our uncertain present. Hammershøi awoke in a period in which he had "no reason" to be, as his admirer Rainer Maria Rilke described artists who did not fit into their era. The future already spoke through him. More than a hundred years in advance, he intuited the spaces in which our souls now wish to reside.

•

The New. What Hammershøi painted in the late nineteenth and early twentieth century was fundamentally new. Sure, he had traveled throughout all of Europe; he had seen the new type of pictures that James McNeill Whistler had developed in England and the works that Eugène Carrière and Pierre Puvis de Chavannes had devised in Paris. Nonetheless, building on his knowledge of these masters of mist and ambiguity, he constructed an oeuvre that was utterly individual.

The truly *new* in art has a unique quality: while it is new in its specific time, it conserves this newness within itself as an indestructible quality for all times. The innovative nature of Giotto, Leonardo, Caravaggio, Goya, Manet, Picasso, or Warhol speaks to us exactly as it already spoke to its contemporaries. Of course, the new *new* is only kindled by other, later, or earlier news. It is the secret formula for an eternal life that is inscribed in these exceptional paintings, a formula that connects them effortlessly with innovators from other times and spaces.

•

Countering Acceleration. Acceleration is the great subject of modernism: it is its secret motor and greatest strength. The twentieth century would be inconceivable without it. Particularly at the turn of the century, it was sweeping everything away with it: people, emotions, certainties, ideologies, nations—and ultimately utopias as well. It was the dawning of a new era, the dawning of a new psychology, a new global economy, a new understanding of gender, and, of course, also the dawning of a new art. Yet Hammershøi resisted its pull like no other. Time was racing, the world was going out of joint, yet Hammershøi resisted. His lifespan, from his birth in 1864 to his death in 1916, covers perhaps the most radical period that the art of modernity ever experienced. Yet Hammershøi responded to it with a radical refusal: when the tempo around him picked up, he put the brakes on; when the Expressionists' colors exploded onto the canvas, he continued to paint in white and gray; when others turned to nature, he stayed at home. Hammershøi continued to paint his interiors in Copenhagen, regardless of whether Symbolism, Neo-Impressionism, Jugendstil, Expressionism, Cubism, or Futurism was being established around him as the expression of the era. While Hammershøi saw it all, he also realized that his path was a different one. This force of resistance, this singular resilience against the course of time gives his pictures their internal power.

Our present view of art history allows us to recognize the exceptional nature of this painter long after his death. He anticipated the atmosphere of René Magritte's mysterious interiors as well as Oscar Schlemmer's chiseled back views. The magic of the forlornness in pictures by Andrew Wyeth or Edward Hopper, too, seems to derive from Hammershøi's works, even if these artists can hardly have known him. The blurriness, the quality of recollection, and the deliberate renunciation of bright colors ultimately find a fitting continuation in Gerhard Richter's painted photographs.

Hammershøi brought time to a standstill in his works, until in the long subsequent century, time created a new art of which he had dreamed long before. Hammershøi even intuited our longings long before they arose: precisely because his pictures are about what is hidden—that is, timeless tales about the unsayable—do they tell us so much in our era that has no secrets.

•

Contemporaneity. The word *contemporaneity* refers to the understanding that people of the same era share a realm of experience, undergo the same events, and partake of a common awareness of life. There is a sense of kinship within a synchronous period. Hammershøi's pictures show, however, that shared experiences may also be recounted as a feeling for life that transcends periods and allow us to surmise and remember although we have not lived through it ourselves.

No artist rises through his own power from the depths of having been subsumed to the surface of another era, another century: rediscovery is not a coincidence, but a deliberate action on the part of the present moment at hand. We only rediscover things that satisfy our current needs, things in which we recognize the present day and our longings, things that already contain elements of our era. Through rediscovery we project the past onto our present. The present in which Hammershøi poses his great questions to his time so silently and insistently—the question of the mystery behind everything, of the position of women, of the survival of humanity, of the realm between dream and reality, and of the pull of introverted melancholy—is the present inscribed in his past. It is a present that our viewing today instantly reactivates, making it "now" all over again.

•

Vermeer's Breath. Hammershøi's most important role model was Jan Vermeer, especially his picture *Girl Reading a Letter at an Open Window* (fig. 1). The held breath that is tangible in Vermeer's interiors, the charged atmosphere of the rooms, the silent energy of the seventeenth-century master from Delft: this was precisely the mysterious aura that Hammershøi wanted to transport into his own time.

There is a loud tradition in the history of art, consisting of artists such as Peter Paul Rubens, Caravaggio, Francisco de Goya, Eugène Delacroix, and Pablo Picasso, who use colors and gestures and compositions to make a ruckus. This did not interest Hammershøi. He stands in the long tradition of silence in the history of art, which began with Cimabue, with Italian painting of the quattrocento—particularly Piero della Francesca—and continued with Chardin,

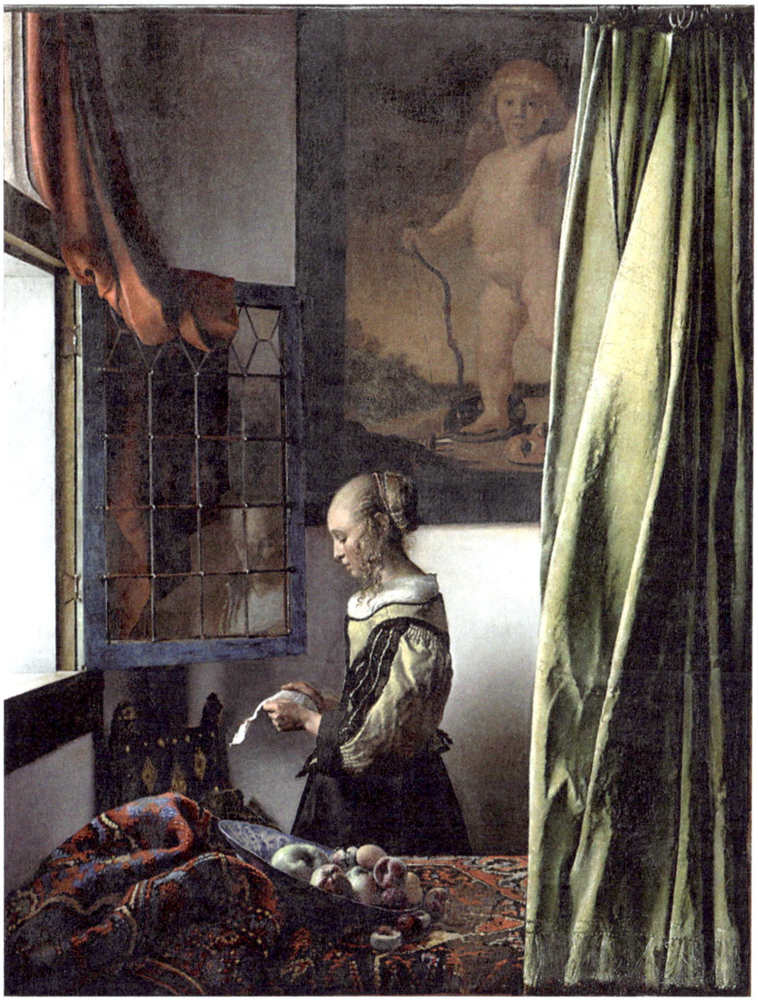

fig. 1

Johannes Vermeer
Girl Reading a Letter at an Open Window, ca. 1657–59
Oil on canvas
32 5/8 × 25 3/8 inches (83 × 64.5 cm)
Gemäldegalerie Alte Meister, Staatliche Kunstsammlungen Dresden

Pieter de Hooch, and Vermeer. After Hammershøi, it would develop into the intensive and yet reserved compositions of Piet Mondrian and Giorgio Morandi. What can one know? What can one see? Can painting be more than the transfer of visual information? These are the looming questions of silent painting—ones that Hammershøi raises anew in each of his pictures.

However, unlike Vermeer, whose isolated figures are charged and challenged through subtle metaphoric and symbolic illusions within the interior, Hammershøi sobers them up. As if to rid them of their last emotions and temporal references, Hammershøi puts his figures under a sort of hypnosis, into a trance. At some point, not only the thoughts of his figures but also the furniture and spaces themselves are transformed into a state of intangibility—into a dream.

When Hammershøi moved to Strandgade 30 in Copenhagen in 1898, he built a timeless home for himself and his wife, Ida. Opposing the period's overstuffed taste for brown wood paneling and heavy furniture, he reconstructed rooms of the Dutch seventeenth century. He had everything painted pastel and gray and selected furniture of the Biedermeier era, which had just fallen out of fashion. He built himself a perfectly sealed capsule while all around it, modernisms' troops heeded the command to charge. Hammershøi's art, like Vermeer's in his time, was downright aggressive about being regressive. This is why it appears to us now to be so subtly progressive.

Hammershøi's life was as silent as his art. He completed his studies, married, and moved into an apartment, which he painted. Then he moved into a different apartment, which he also painted. He had no children and did not fight in any wars. He often sat in a chair for hours, staring at the wall. He knew every detail of the chest of drawers and the piano; every cold draft. Occasionally he went on a trip—much more often than one might assume—traveling to Paris, London, Berlin, and Rome. But everything that he saw and experienced there he seems to have pushed away and left outside the door when he sat down at his easel at Strandgade 30 and pondered. This enabled him to create an atmosphere of maximal intensification, concentration, and silence in his art. Hammershøi charged his interiors with everything that he left out: they are acts of resistance against the world forcing itself upon you. They still have this power.

Time stands still and the air is stuffy in Hammershøi's pictures. The world momentarily holds its breath, and the figures who stand inside or stroll through these pictures also remain silent—especially his wife, Ida. Not a word is uttered; instead, there is devotion, amazement, emotion. It does not take long for Hammershøi's silence to calm our restless eyes and bewitch us with the infinite longing and melancholy that strangely radiates from all the twilights of his pictures.

•

Ghosts. Hammershøi transforms the people in his works into timid ghosts. His interiors could be stage sets for the plays of his Scandinavian contemporaries Henrik Ibsen and August Strindberg, diffuse invocations of absence.

In Strindberg's *Ghost Sonata* from 1908, a group gathers in a formal dining room. The figures are caught in this space with their invented histories—they are unable to escape back to life. Ibsen's *Ghosts* (1881) is about the memories that overshadow the present and lead to the condition that "we are all of us ghosts." It is not merely old thoughts haunting people, but entire rooms that are full of ghosts—ghosts that are "gliding" everywhere: people, feelings, threats. That explains why "we are, one and all, so pitifully afraid of the light." This is the fear of both Stindberg's and Hammershøi's imprisoned figures. They are so afraid of the light because they would have to become human beings if they left their dim apartments. This fear is what makes Hammershøi's works so uncanny and so modern: we want to turn the handles of his white doors and look behind them, but we do not know what lies behind them: paradise or hell.

•

The Role of Women. The figures in Hammershøi's works are almost always female, and one woman is almost always his model: Ida, his wife, whom he married early and whom he portrayed from behind in their shared apartment in countless paintings. Wearing the ideal body of the quattrocento like a veil around herself, she recalls the solemn figures of Masolino or Perugino.

Of course, Vermeer also painted many women, and there are many images of Caspar David Friedrich's wife, Caroline, especially the famous painting *Woman at the Window* (1822), in which she is shown from behind (fig. 2). This work, which Hammershøi encountered early, would influence him for the rest of his life. We see Ida time and again in the pictures: she stands pensively with a bowl under her arm, reads a newspaper, and stands before a piano—or she sleepwalks through the spaces of their shared apartment. Is she lost? Is she deep in thought? Is she happy? Is she sick of life? We do not know.

All the paintings of Ida are like stills from an endless film without a plot. This aspect is reminiscent of one of the most famous photo series of recent art history, Cindy Sherman's *Untitled Film Stills*, which were created about a hundred years after Hammershøi's first

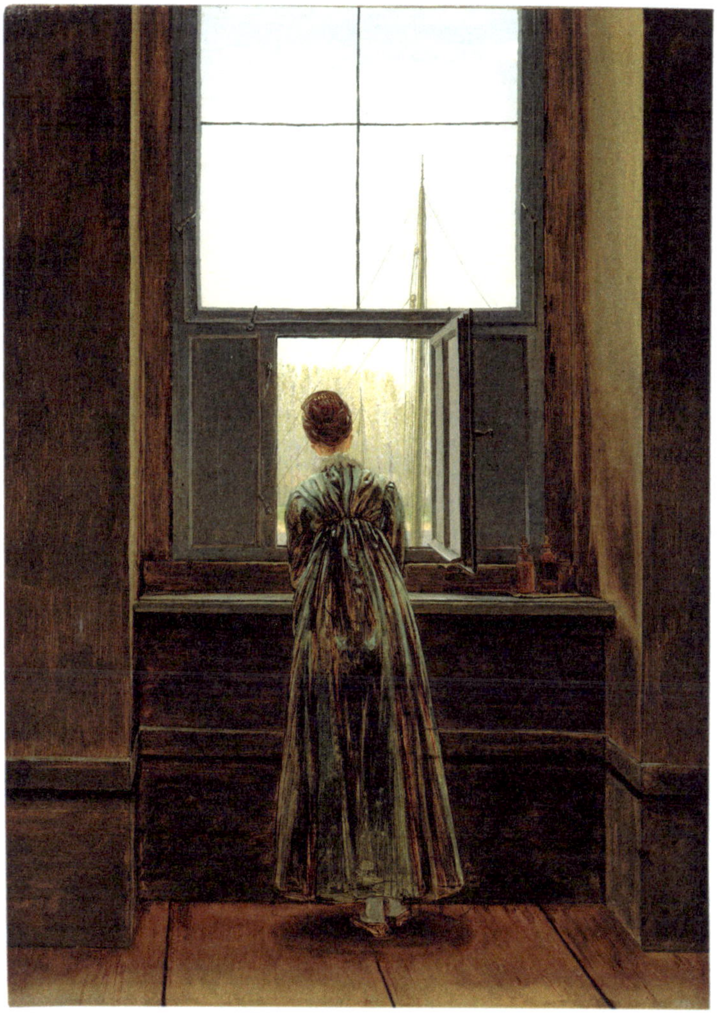

fig. 2

Caspar David Friedrich
Woman at the Window, 1822
Oil on canvas
17 ¾ × 12 ⅞ inches (45 × 32.7 cm)
Alte Nationalgalerie, Staatliche Museen zu Berlin

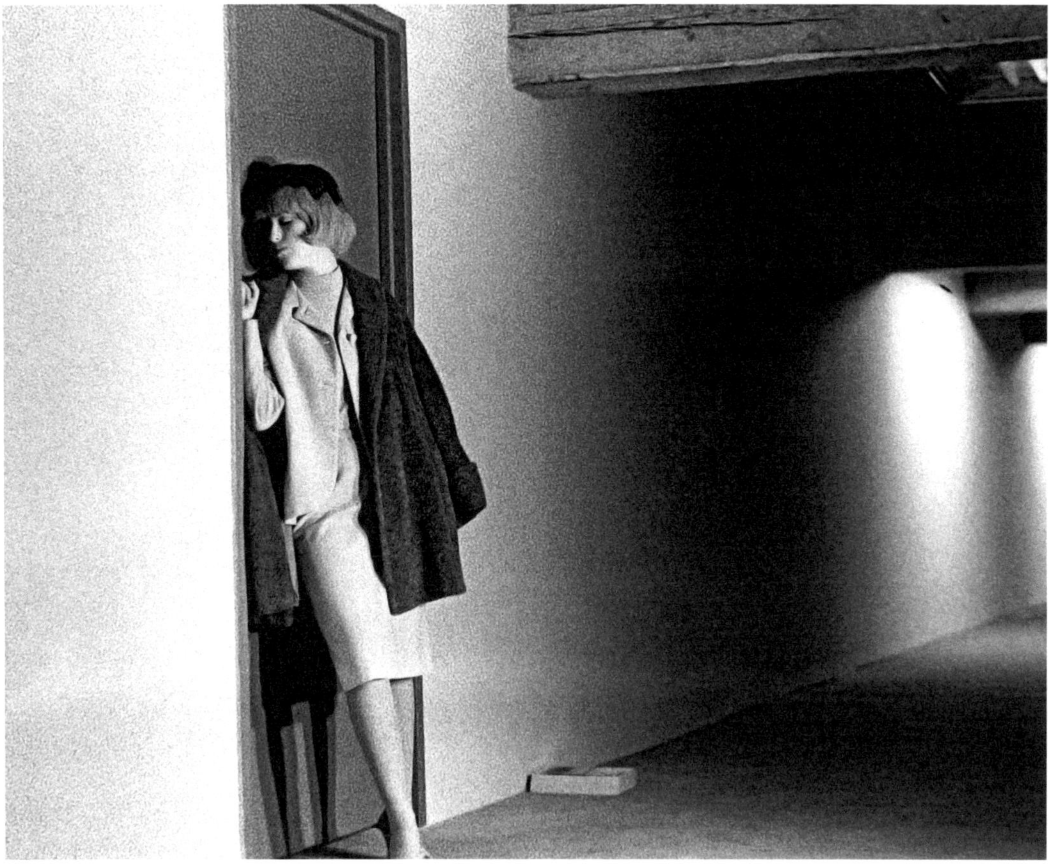

fig. 3

Cindy Sherman
Untitled Film Still #4, 1977
Gelatin silver print
8 × 10 inches (20.3 × 25.4 cm)

paintings, in the time between 1977 and 1980 (fig. 3). The photos appear to be stills from an old film in which the female protagonist, who is always Sherman herself, slips into different poses and roles; the narrative, however, is unclear and can only be completed in the act of viewing. While Sherman's goal was to create pictures that are virtually blank and stop just short of fiction, she also plays with collective forms of femininity and domesticity. Hammershøi, a century earlier, made his wife, Ida, enact a similar game with female identity—and yet he only allows her to play the role that she would be playing anyway. It is interesting that Sherman stages her figures (and, in turn, herself) in 1940s interiors to make use of old stereotypes, while Hammershøi casts his wife back into the world of the 1840s through the Biedermeier furniture and her simple clothing. In neither case is anything explained or narrated; everything is opaque.

Although Hammershøi's wife may be near the piano, she does not play; although she stands near a table, she does not touch her teacup. There is no action; there is only the possibility of an action. It can be intuited that in her thoughts, the possibility slowly becomes an impossibility.

This aspect of making the inner, psychological world visible links Hopper's paintings to those of Hammershøi. Hopper, too, only had one model, his wife, Josephine; in the case of this couple, too, revolving around each other for decades led to an oeuvre in which intimacy often verges on the claustrophobic.

Hopper has a similar predilection for interior space and the protection against the threats of the outside world that he extends to his depicted wife. Only the light is allowed to penetrate this insular world (fig. 4). Hopper's wife sits on the bed, on the sofa, in a bar—although the world has become more modern, our thoughts have not. Who am I? What is my role in this world? Why should I ever go outside again? Is isolation not also salvation? The deep melancholy of these eternal questions wafts directly from Hammershøi's Old Europe to Hopper's New World.

•

Repetition Compulsions. During Hammershøi's lifetime, Sigmund Freud developed the concept of *Wiederholungszwang*, or "repetition compulsion," to describe the manic impulse to repeat even painful dreams or actions. Hammershøi's repetition compulsion consisted in staring at his apartment on Strandgade and painting it repeatedly. This aspect is central to the modernity of his oeuvre, since this compulsive quality quite convincingly subverts the seeming harmlessness of his works.

Like a photographer who obsessively photographs the same motif or a musician who plays the same note, Hammershøi devoted himself to his apartment. He often took care to make small changes, moving a piece of furniture aside or pulling up a chair, closing one door or opening another. But it is these small variations that reveal the modernity of this seriality, which Monet initiated with his grainstacks. It is always Ida whom Hammershøi—as in a dollhouse—places in a different room and associates with ever-changing accessories from a small array of household effects. This is so new because the pictures entirely lack a sense of event; it is the absence of an event that makes them so exciting.

In his spaces, Hammershøi seems to have repealed the outside world. The wishes and fears of his wife and his era are sealed inside his pictures as in vessels. This condensation of the atmosphere and

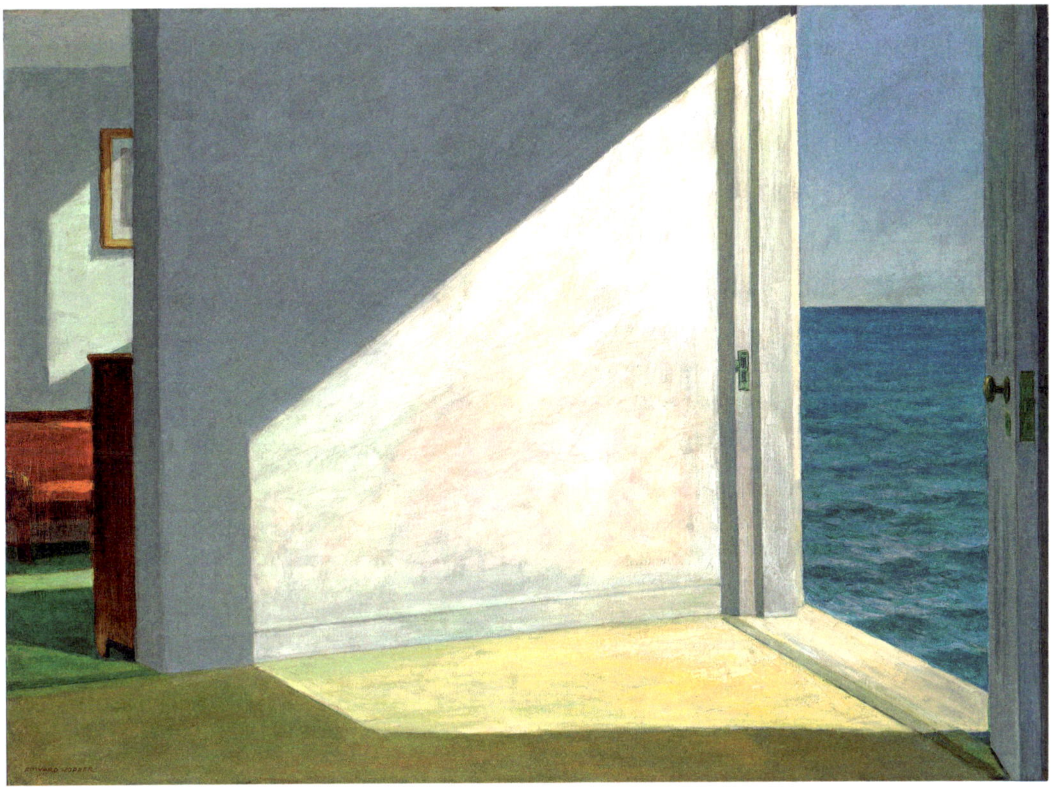

fig. 4

Edward Hopper
Rooms by the Sea, 1951
Oil on canvas
29 1/4 × 40 inches (74.3 × 101.6 cm)
Yale University Art Gallery, New Haven

motifs links his work so plausibly to Morandi's still lifes. Working in his isolated studio, Morandi depicted the world's diversity and its axial shifts purely through the rearrangement of bottles and jugs on a table (fig. 5). In this ostensible uneventfulness, the smallest nuance becomes a sensation and the monotony of the muted palette recalls Hammershøi's reduction of colors—even if Morandi's colors tend to be yellowish and reddish, whereas in Hammershøi's works they at most take on a brownish tone in the dull twilight of the indoor space that connects both artists' pictures. Hammershøi paints the door and the piano as seriously and attentively as if they were people, just as Morandi does with the jug and bottle: the reduced world of objects, for those who are able to look, becomes an infinite universe.

Morandi's and Hammershøi's pallid pictures, frozen in the depiction of a moment, nonetheless challenge the eye. One searches for nuances and deviations. The obsessive recurrence of a motif, in alliance with a barely perceptible modulation of light, conceals the true content: the complete rejection of classical narrative structure. This endows Hammershøi's compositions—including the spaces and people depicted—with the air of an eternally valid ideology. German poet Rainer Maria Rilke described it after encountering Hammershøi and his art as follows: "His work is long and slow, and whensoever one studies it, that moment will always be an occasion for speaking about the important and essential in art."

•

Oyster Shells. Hammershøi's subdued palette suited his subdued surroundings: the white doors and windows, the gray walls and ceilings, the warm honey-brown of the Biedermeier and Empire

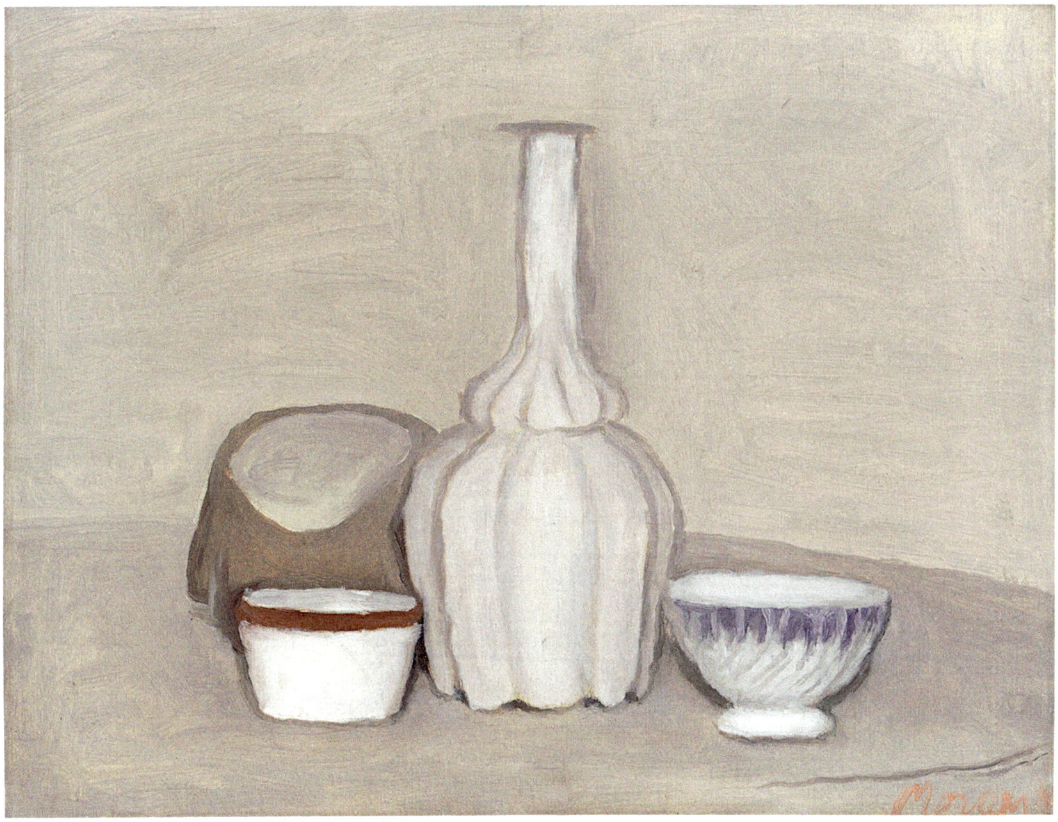

fig. 5

Giorgio Morandi
Natura morta, 1946
Oil on canvas
14 × 18 ¾ inches (35.5 × 47.5 cm)
Private collection

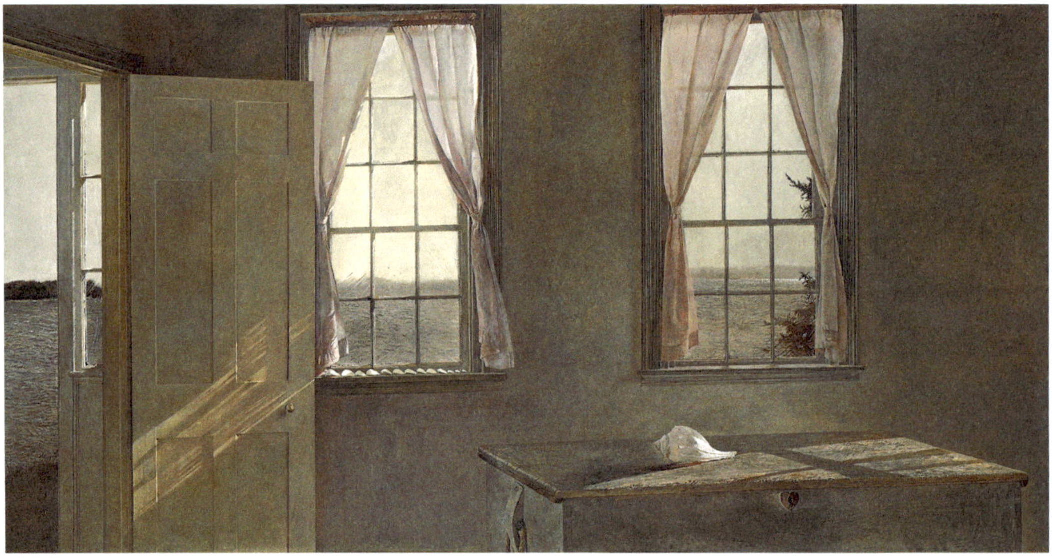

fig. 6

Andrew Wyeth
Her Room, 1963
Tempera on panel
24 ¾ × 48 inches (62.9 × 121.9 cm)
Farnsworth Art Museum, Rockland, Maine

furniture. These are his colors; he did not need more. When he looked out at the city, he only needed gray and the milkiness of a mottled white: a magnificent silver-gray and over it, repeatedly, delicate tones like powdery snow. When he went out into nature, a bleary, pallid green, as if just before dusk, was added. Nothing more.

Hammershøi's colors, however, consist of an unlimited range of gray tones. When Danish painter Joakim Skovgaard once had the chance to look at Hammershøi's palette, he was captivated by its limitations: "On it there lay four gray and white blobs of color which were scrupulously delimited from each other. The strange thing about them was that there was layer upon layer of color, and that they had been smoothed down into these layers so that it appeared to be four oyster shells lying on the palette." These oyster shells were the basis for the pearls of Hammershøi's art.

The powdery daubs of paint on his canvases are rhythmized through light, which serves as the secret stage director in each of his pictures. This provokingly diffuse light was capable of transforming the spaces of his apartment into ever-changing pictures, due to the time of day, the light's angle of entry, or a cloud's shadow.

This play with the transformative power of light also spread to American modernism, to both Hopper and Andrew Wyeth (fig. 6). Holland Cotter of the *New York Times* asked in complete surprise in 1998, "Is there any real difference between Hammershøi's *Dust Motes Dancing in the Sunbeams* (1900) and one of Mr. Wyeth's Maine farmhouse interiors washed with winter light?" He continued, "Both images traffic in a melancholy sense of the ephemeral, a naturalism of nostalgia."

This treatment of light and the subtle interplay between black and white also connect Hammershøi with the great photographers of his era such as Alfred Stieglitz and Heinrich Kühn. He dematerializes the world through the graininess of his paintings, whose reduced palette and statue-like quality frequently recall early photography. Hammershøi likely often used photographs as the basis for his pictures; he was aware of their special qualities in the reduction of tonality and compositional clarification. This leads directly to the conflation that occurs in Richter's painted photographs of the 1960s: the intangibility that becomes a theme, the desire for unclarity, and especially the silent doubt regarding the medium of photography are congruent with Hammershøi's unspoken doubt about the medium of painting (fig. 7).

•

After the Ball. The enticing and painful silence that envelops each one of Hammershøi's canvases feeds from quiet grief. They are all pictures of farewell. Hammershøi seems to already retreat from the twentieth century although it has not yet even begun. His wife, Ida, too, seems like a memory from a dream that becomes more elusive the more you open your eyes. The rooms of his apartment in Copenhagen, the furniture, each picture feels like a final look back. The anemic grisaille of his palette intensifies this effect.

A final look back—but at what? The rooms are already practically empty and devoid of life. The few landscapes and farms also seem abandoned; no bird flies there anymore and no wind blows, and in the bare streets and weathered houses that he paints outside, no human being seems still to be living. They all have left us.

At that moment of world history when acceleration was rapidly gaining momentum, it seems as if Hammershøi already wanted to paint a world from which the centrifugal forces had ejected

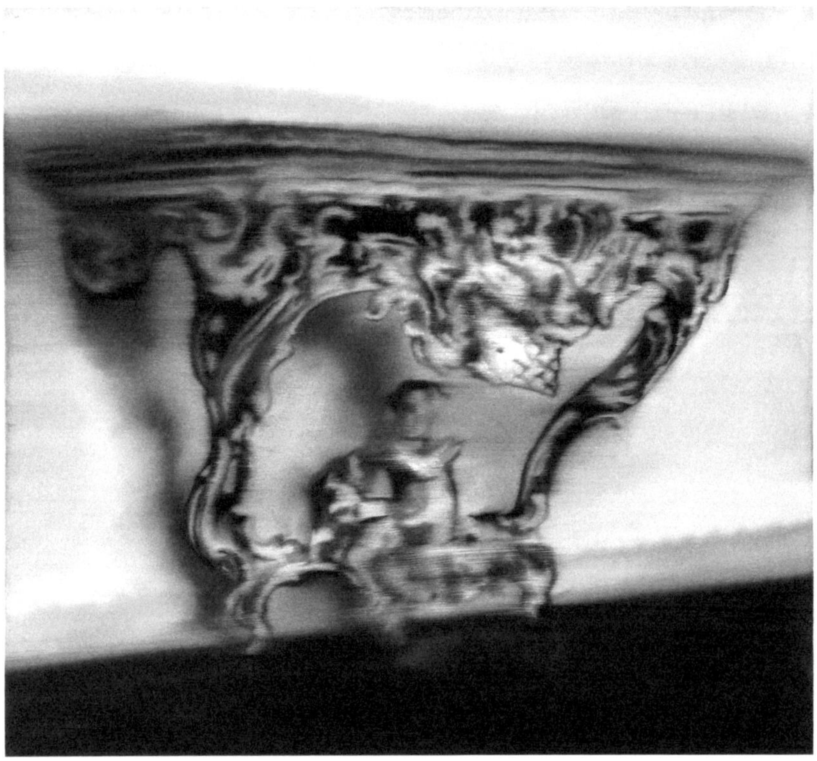

fig. 7

Gerhard Richter
Rococo Table, 1964
Oil on canvas
35 3/8 × 39 3/8 inches (90 × 100 cm)
Private collection

humankind. Only Ida seems to have remained: a last human being whom he paints going through the clean-swept rooms, checking everything one final time before she too must go, treading softly so as not to disturb the final silence that has already descended over everything.

The *Interior of the Great Hall in Lindegaarden* (1909, pp. 72–73), perhaps Hammershøi's boldest picture, tells of this farewell. It is an empty room; only the ornaments on the ceiling and walls still remind us that the space was once teeming with life. The ballroom tells of a world after people, after the last generation, that is, the end of the Anthropocene. Vilhelm Hammershøi conveys the sense that the world has achieved its goal and can finally exist on its own again, immortalizing in every painting the precious moment in which time and eternity touch.

PLATES

Interior with White Door and Yellow Wardrobe, 1886
Oil on canvas
15 3/8 × 14 3/8 inches (39 × 36.5 cm)

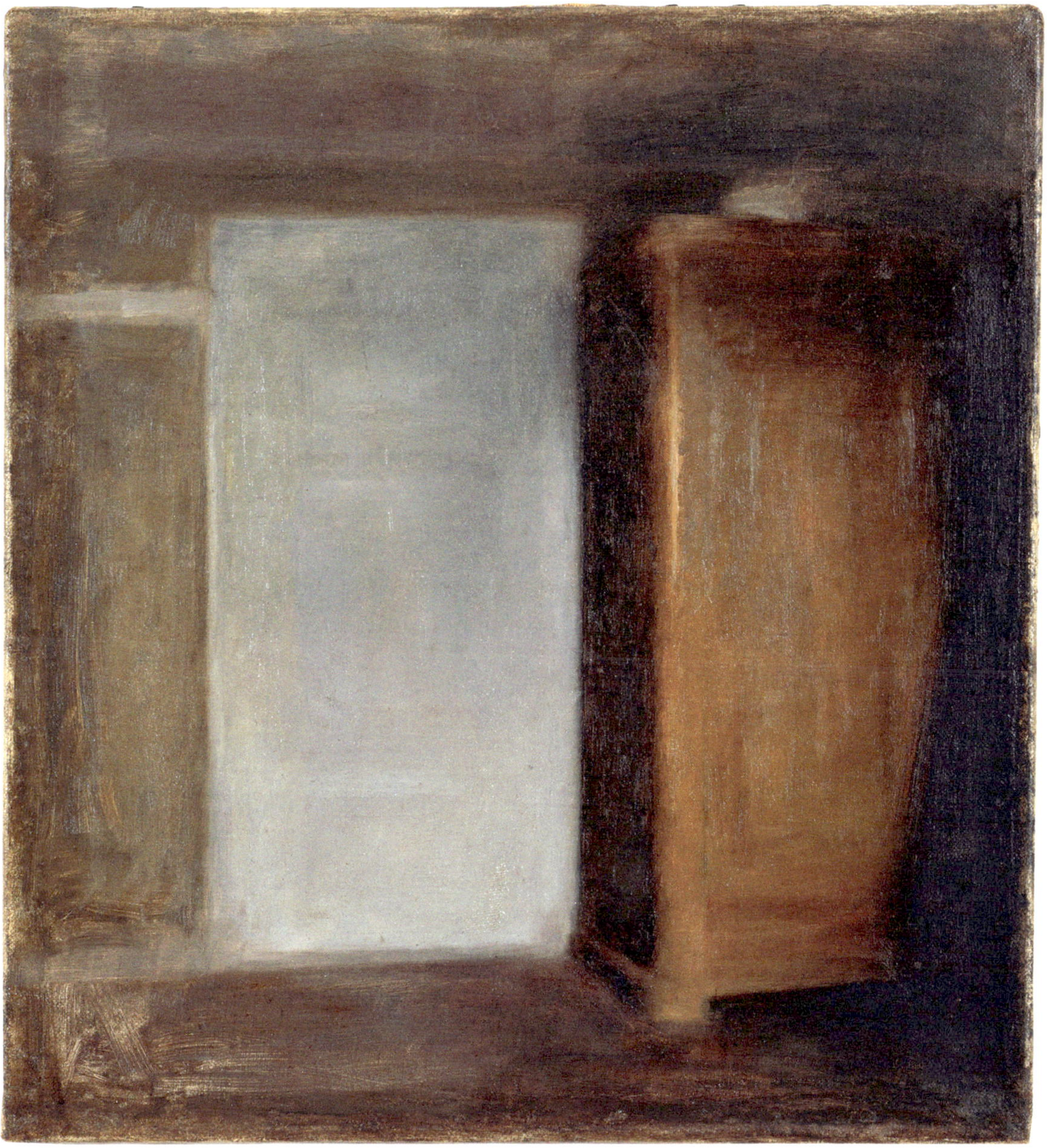

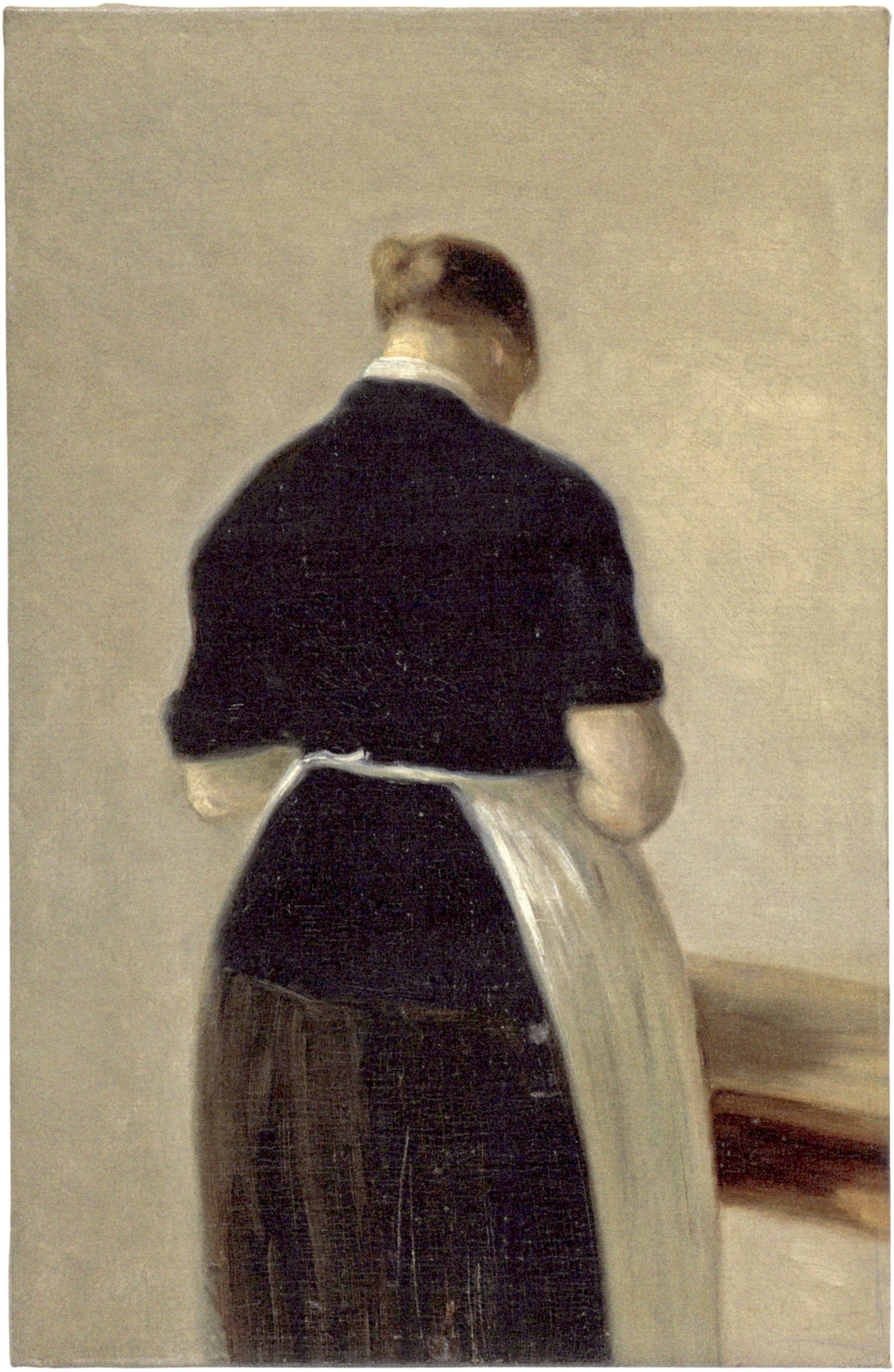

Study of Standing Woman, Seen from Behind, 1884–88
Oil on canvas
21 1/8 × 14 inches (53.7 × 35.6 cm)

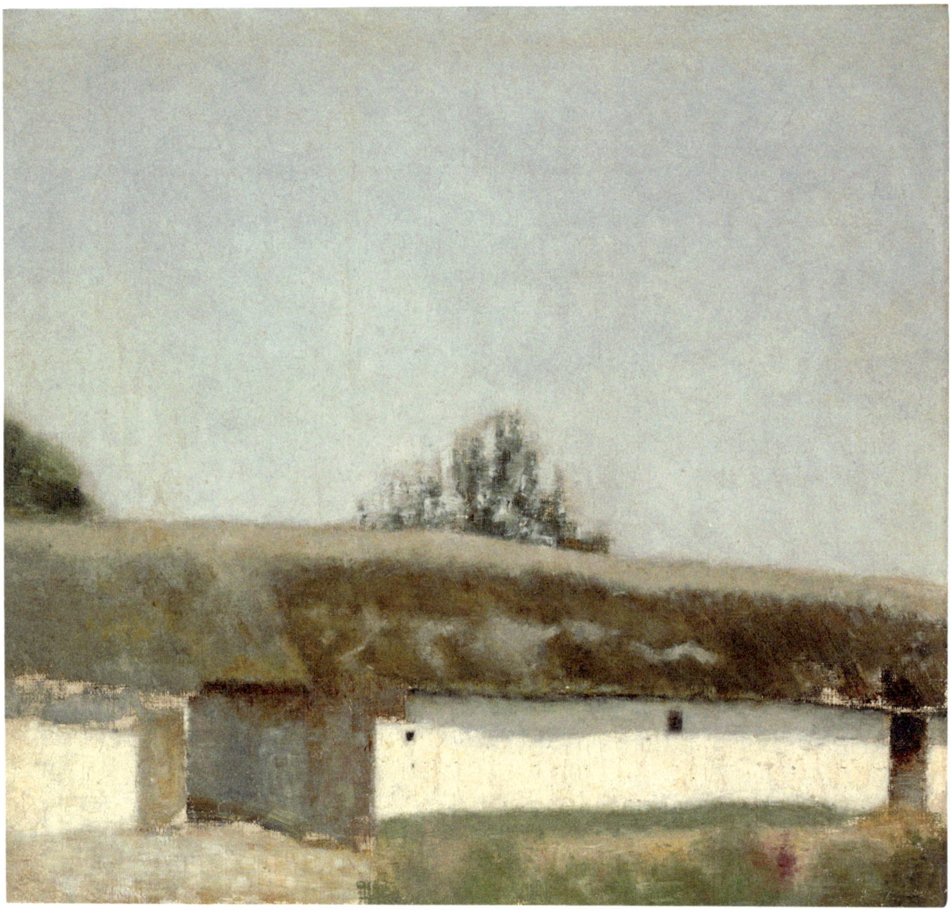

Landscape with a Barn, 1883
Oil on canvas
13 3/8 × 14 1/8 inches (34 × 36 cm)

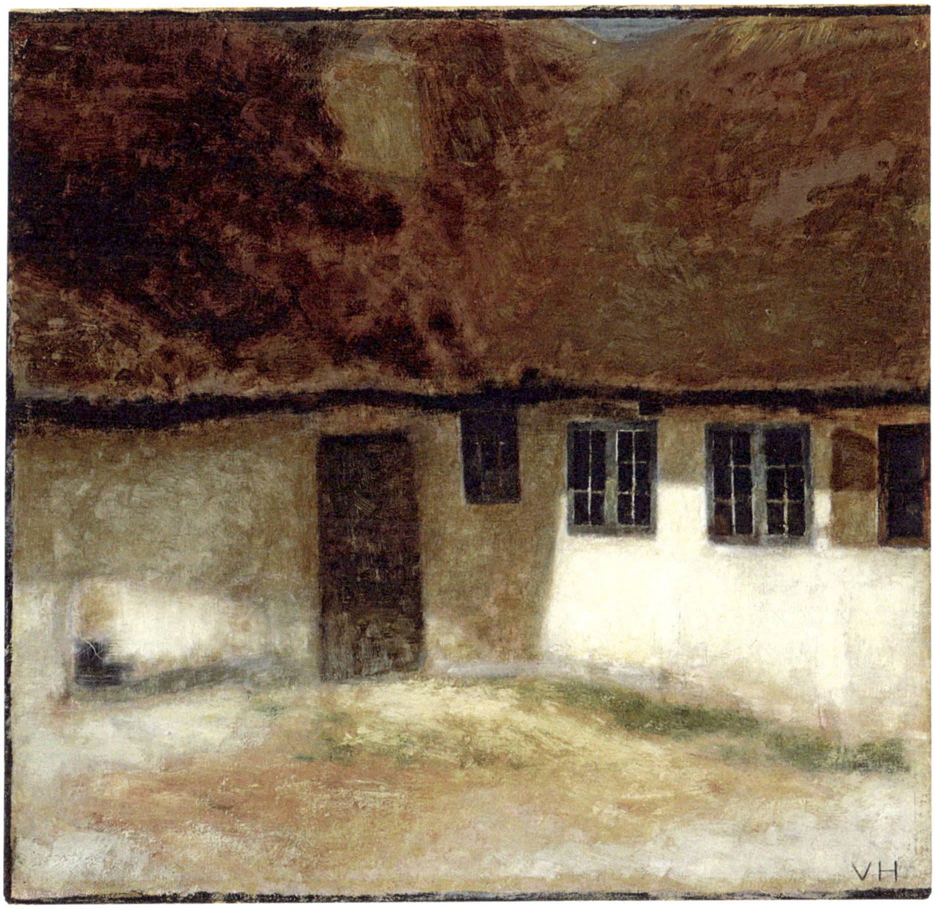

Farmhouse, 1883
Oil on canvas
13 3/8 × 14 1/8 inches (34 × 36 cm)

Interior with a Standing Woman, 1898
Oil on canvas
19 1/8 × 16 3/4 inches (48.5 × 42.4 cm)

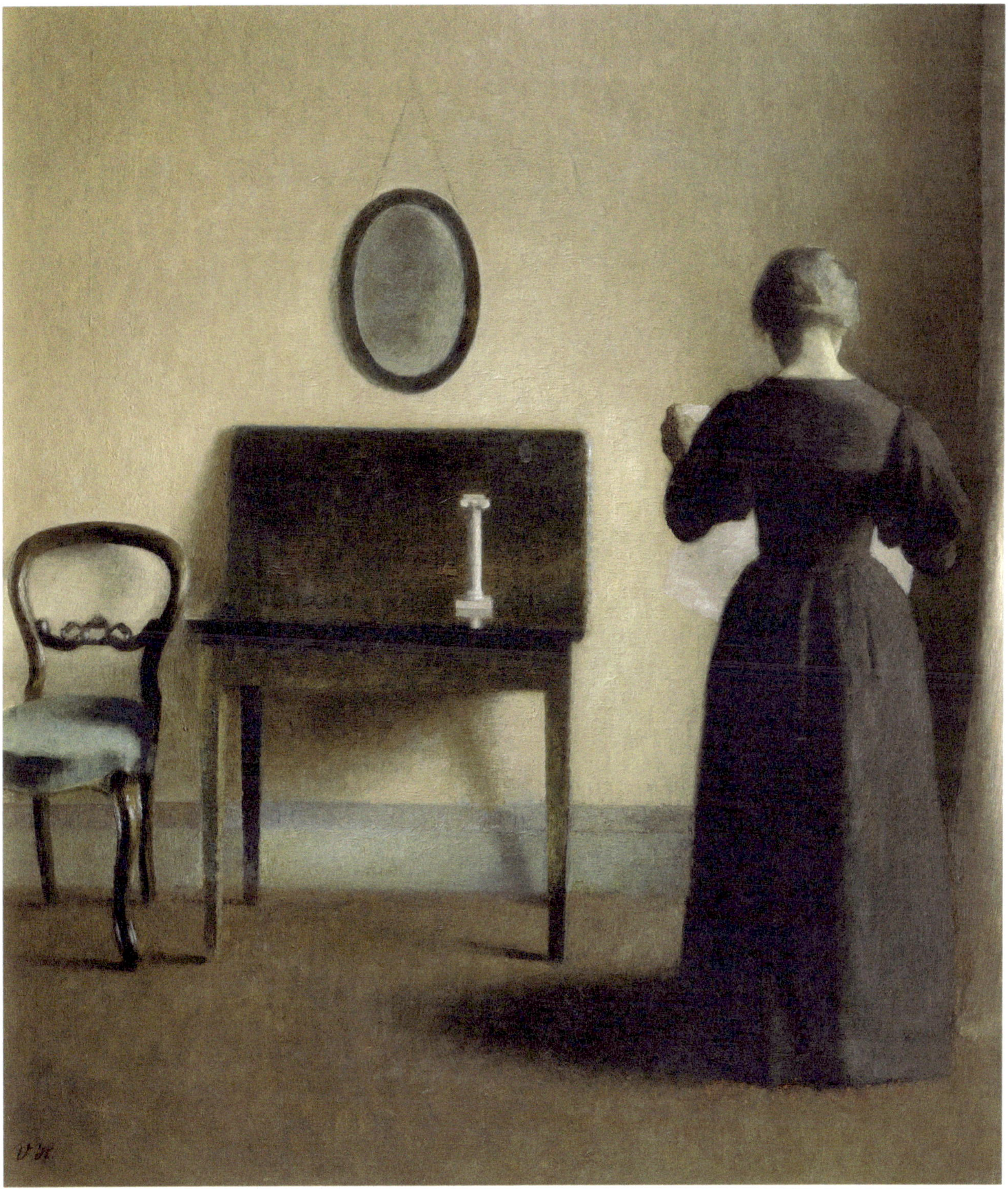

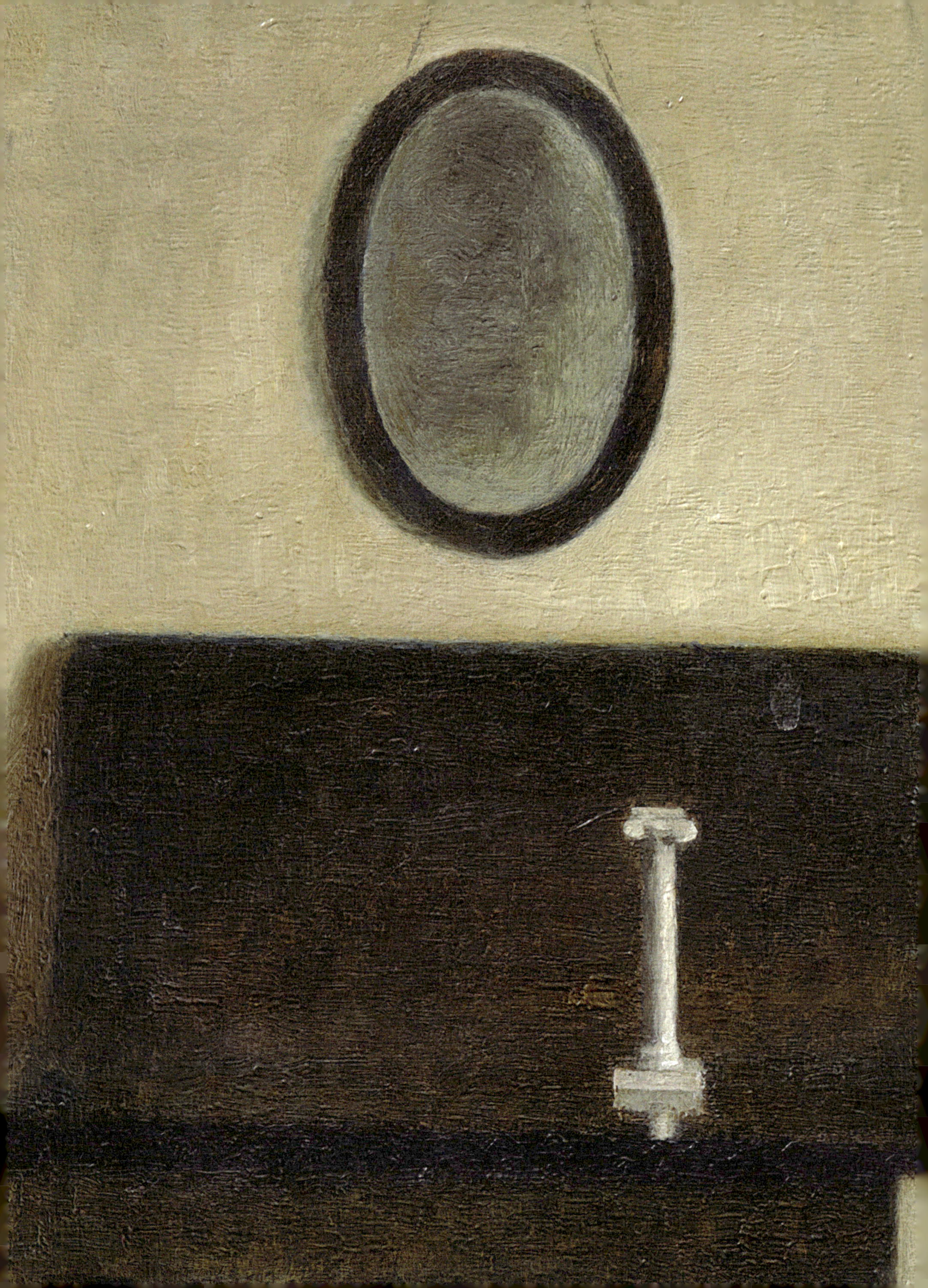

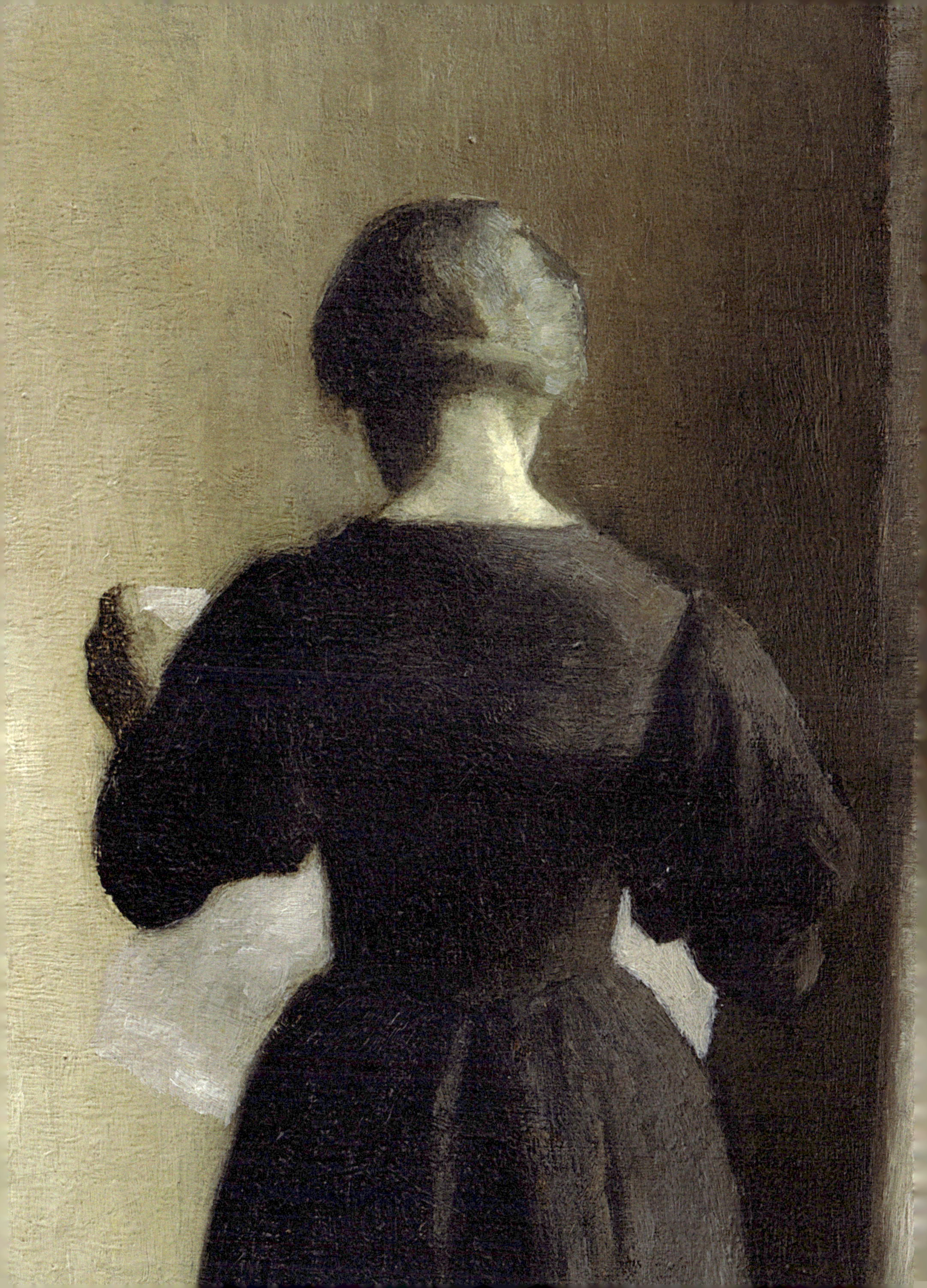

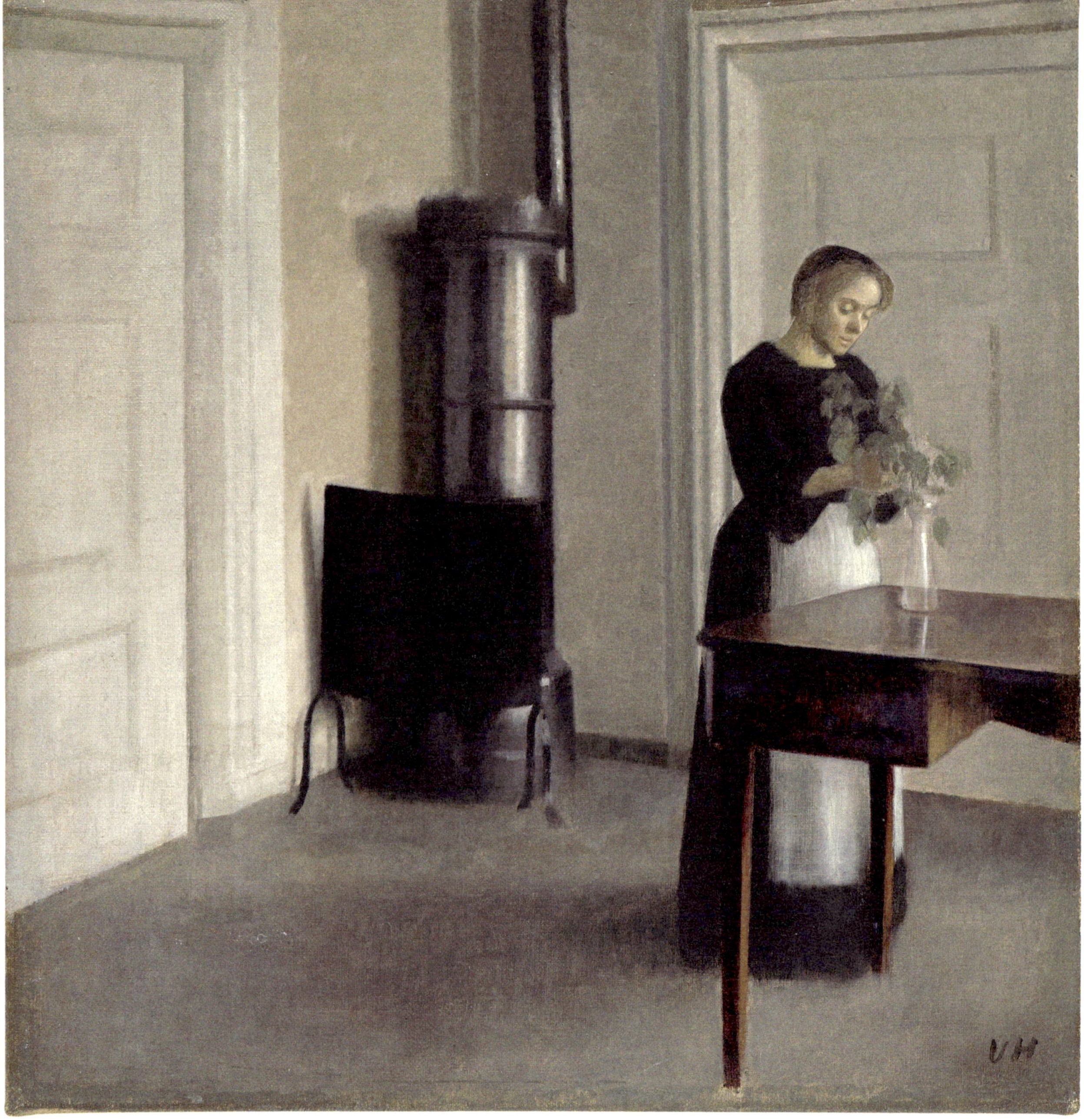
VH

Interior with Woman Placing Branches in Vase on Table, 1900
Oil on canvas
15 ⅞ × 15 ½ inches (40.3 × 39.4 cm)

Interior with a Writing Desk, 1900
Oil on canvas
18 ½ × 18 ⅞ inches (47 × 48 cm)

Interior in London, Brunswick Square, 1912
Oil on canvas
20 ⅞ × 29 ⅞ inches (53 × 76 cm)
↘

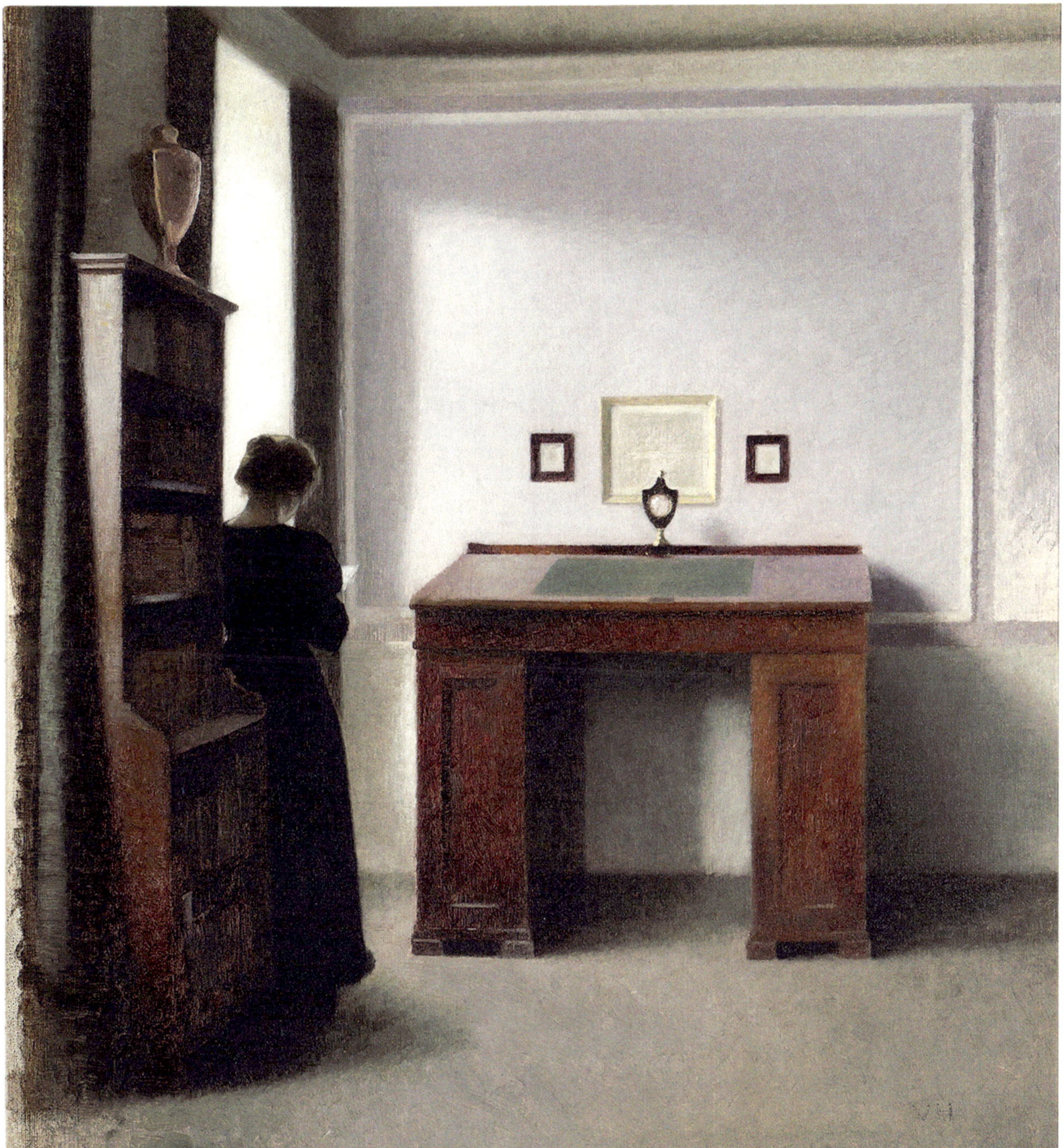

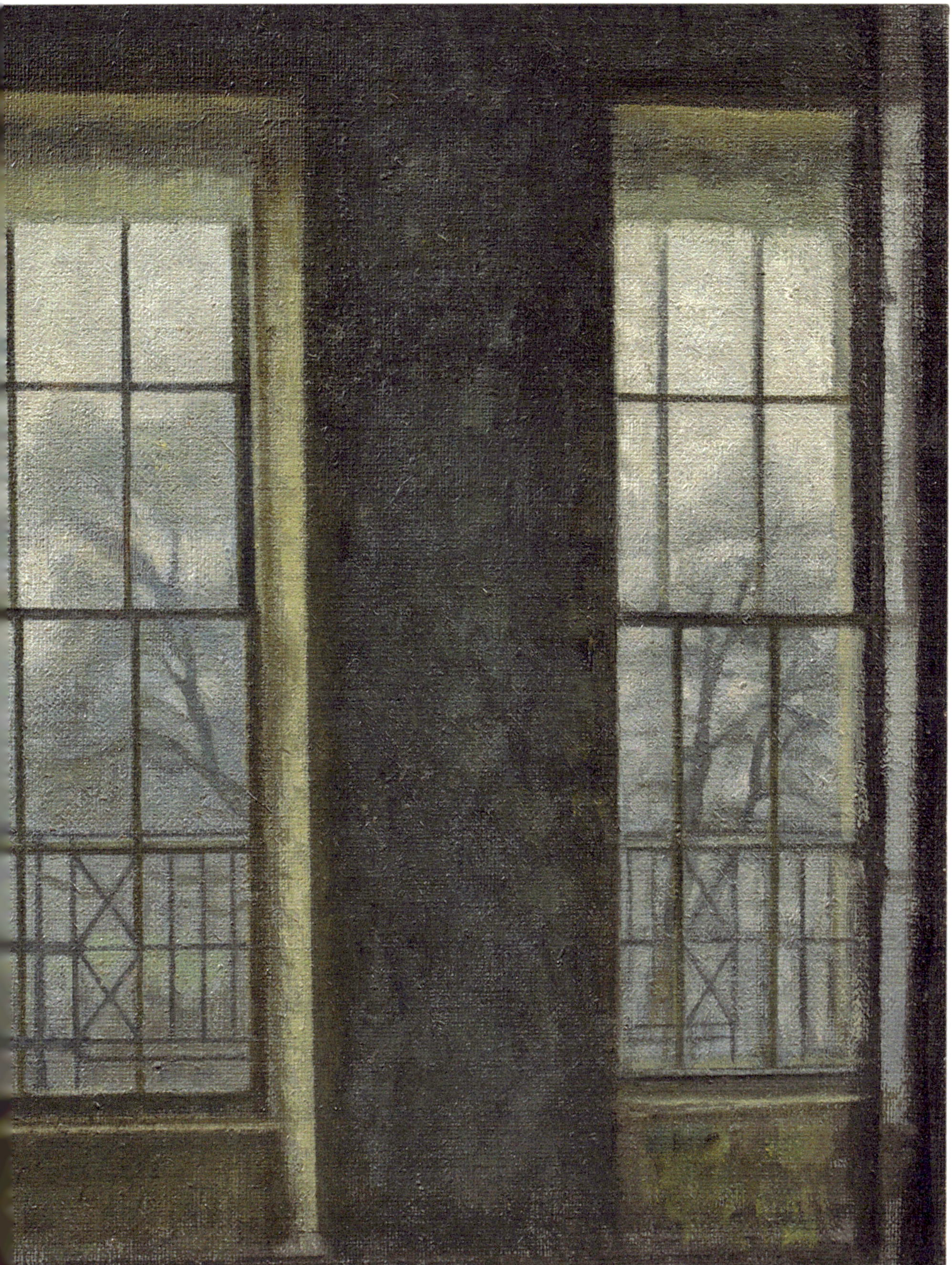

Woman before a Mirror, 1906
Oil on canvas
18 ⅛ × 15 ⅛ inches (46 × 38.5 cm)

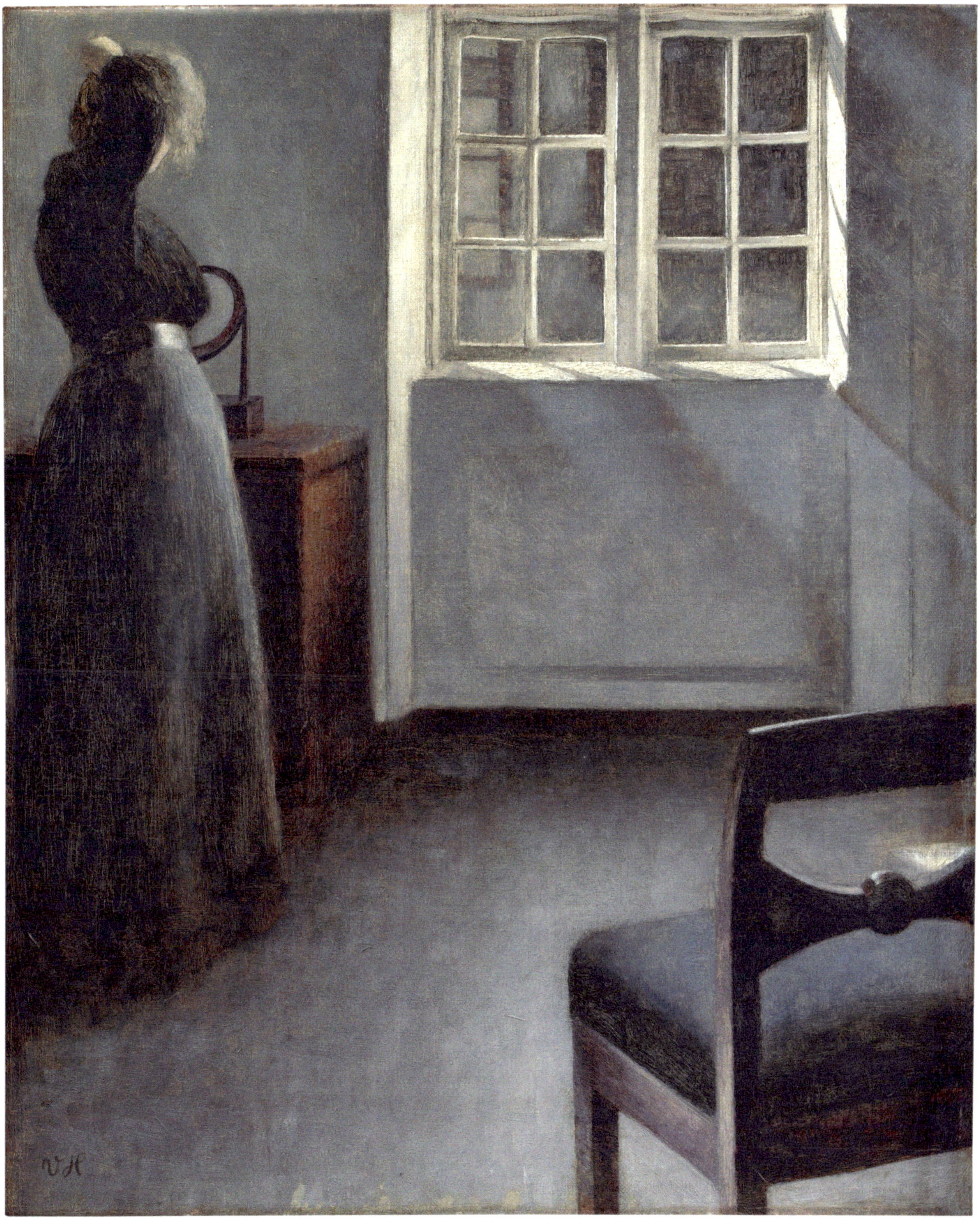

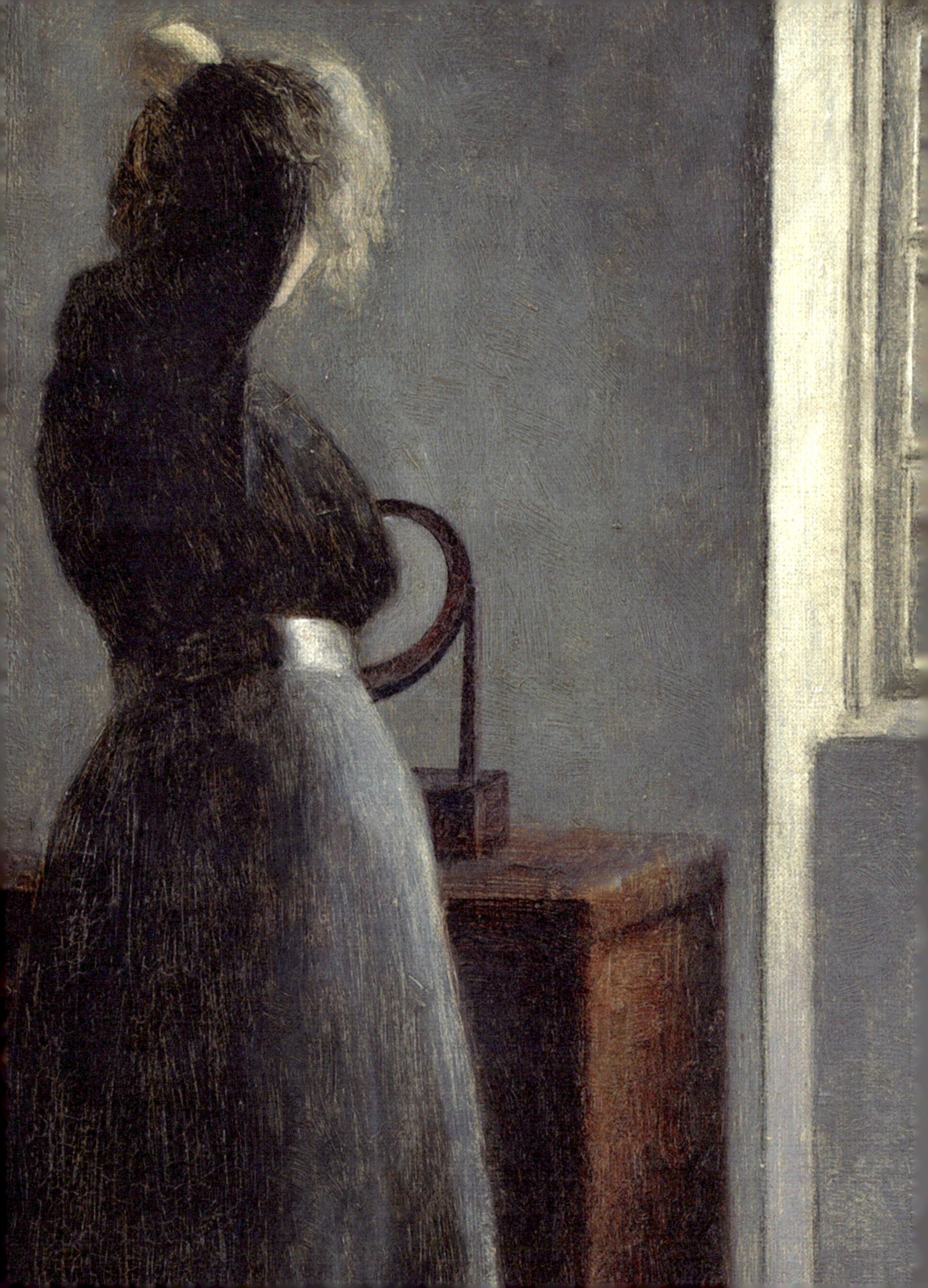

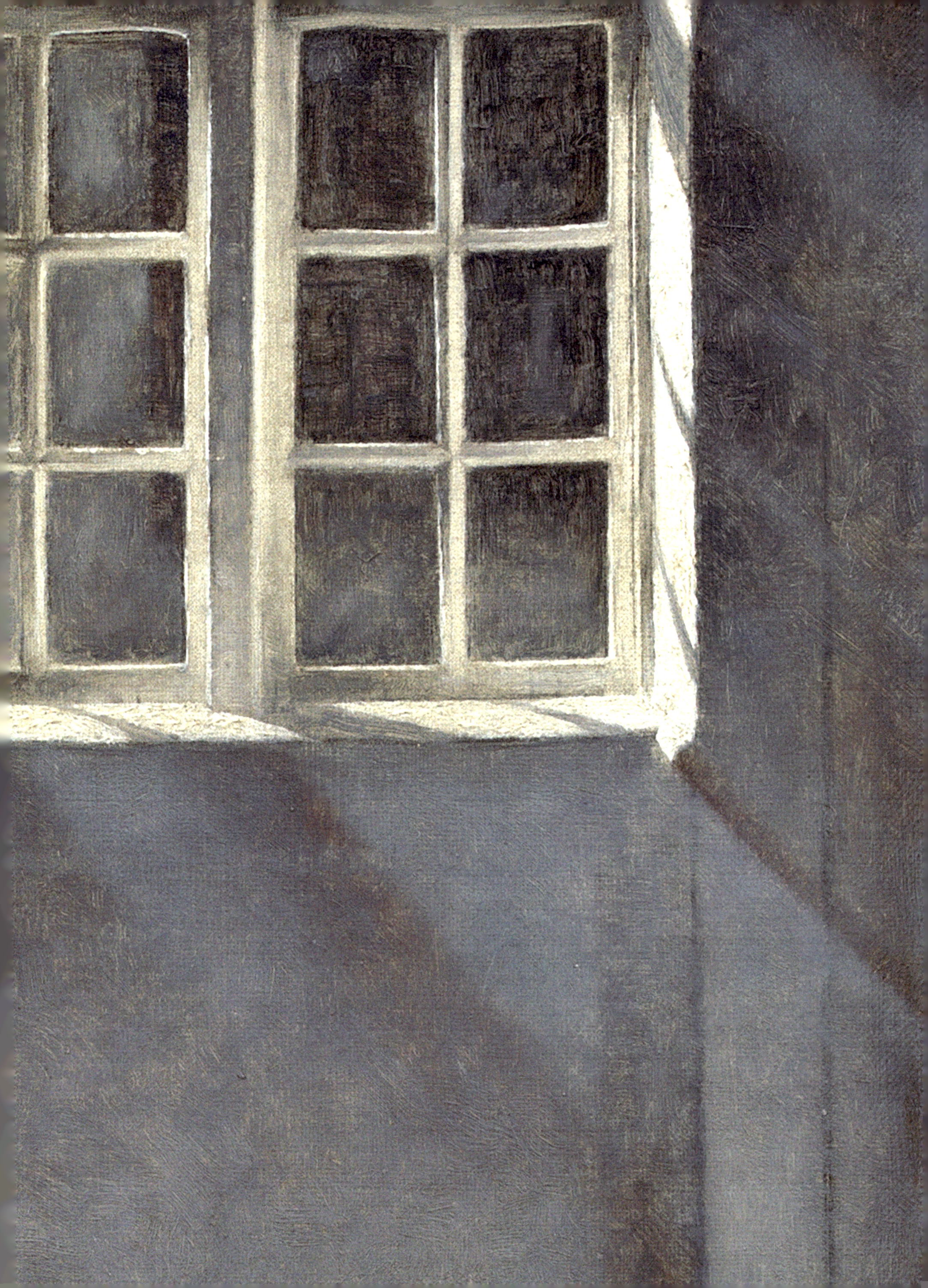

Courtyard Interior at Strandgade 30, ca. 1905
Oil on canvas, mounted on panel
32 × 21½ inches (81.3 × 54.6 cm)

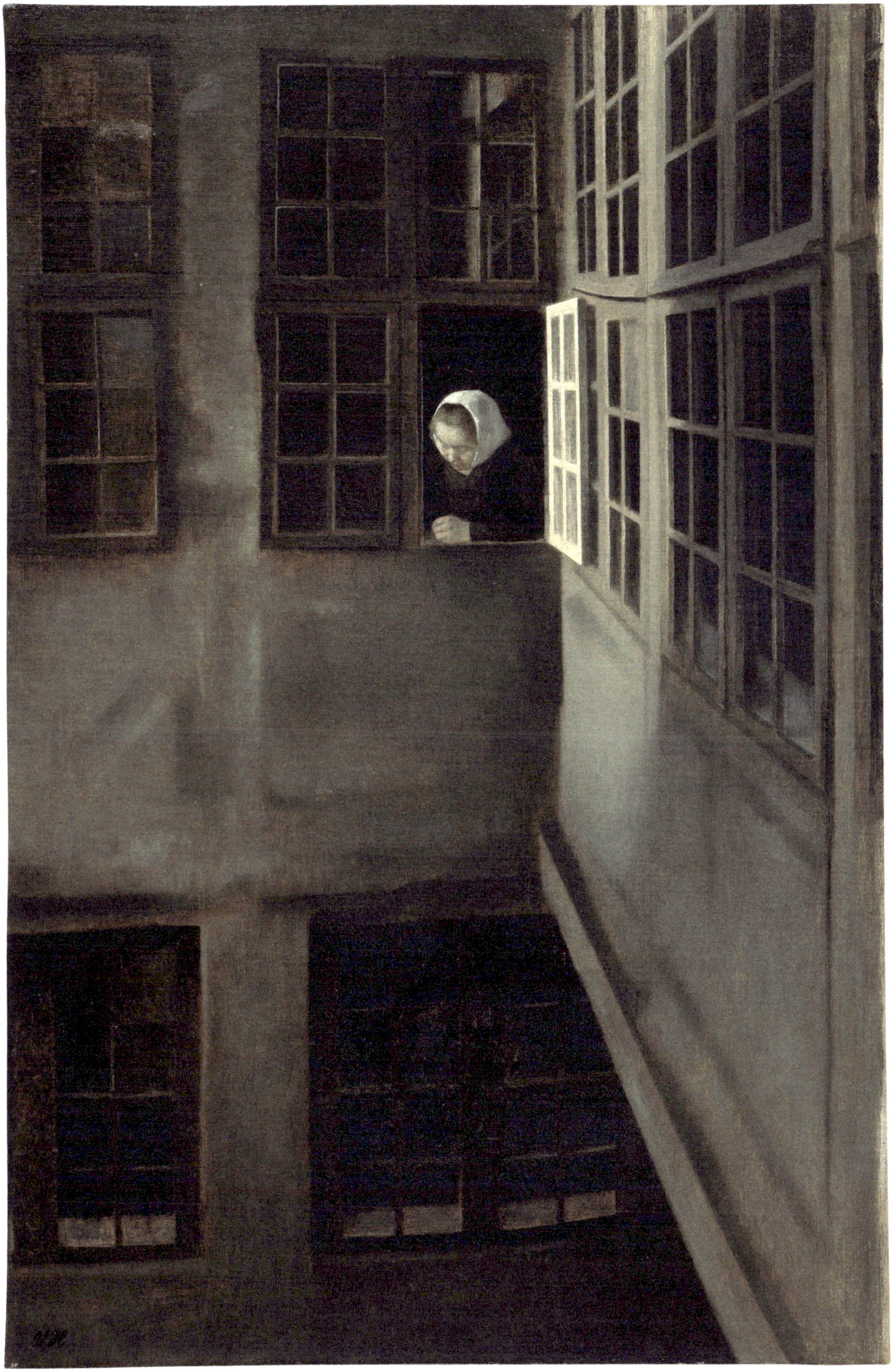

Interior with the Artist's Wife, Seen from Behind, 1901
Oil on canvas
17 ¾ × 15 ⅜ inches (45 × 39 cm)

Interior of the Great Hall in Lindegaarden, 1909
Oil on canvas
30 ⅜ × 46 ½ inches (77 × 118 cm)
↘

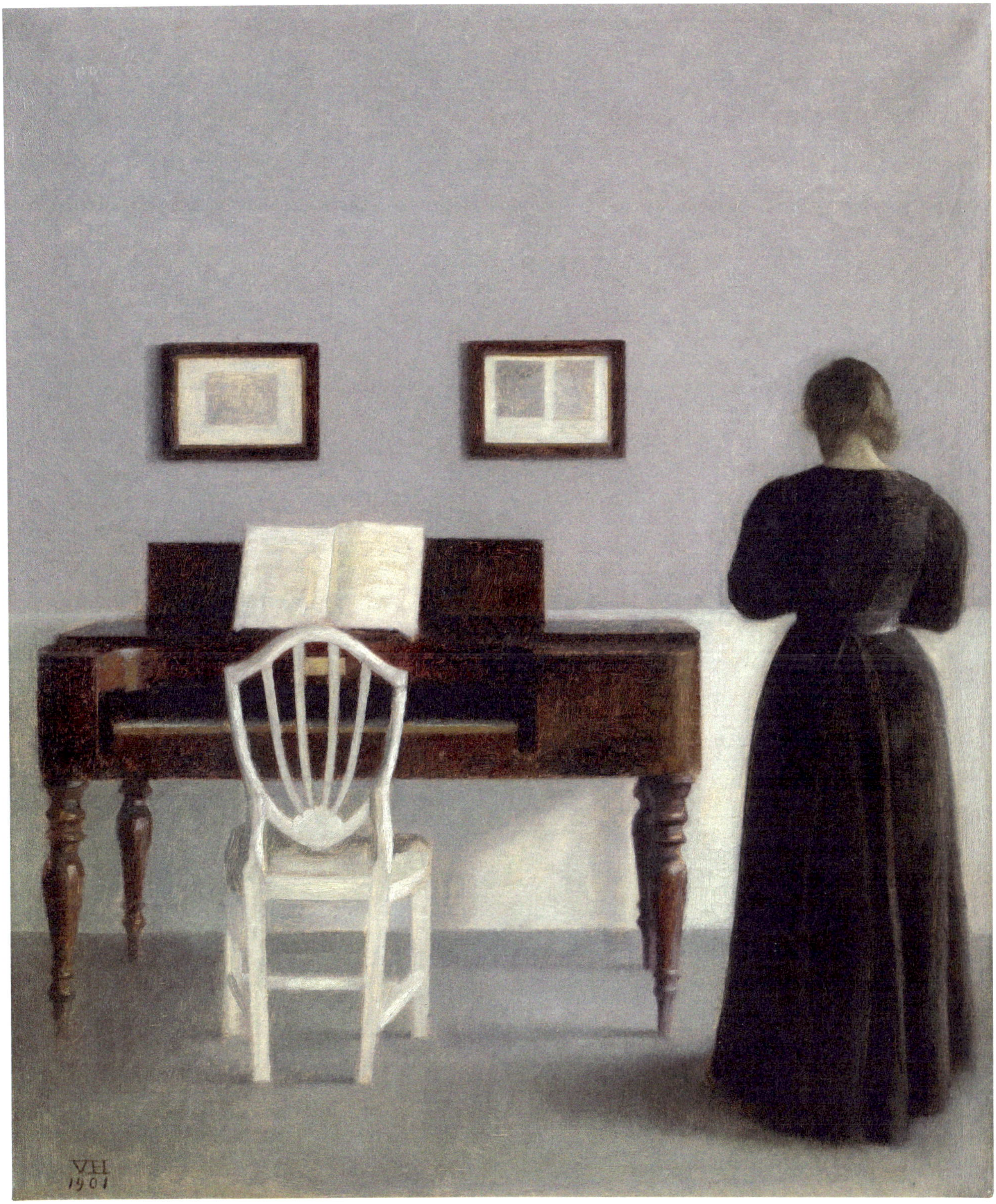
VH
1901

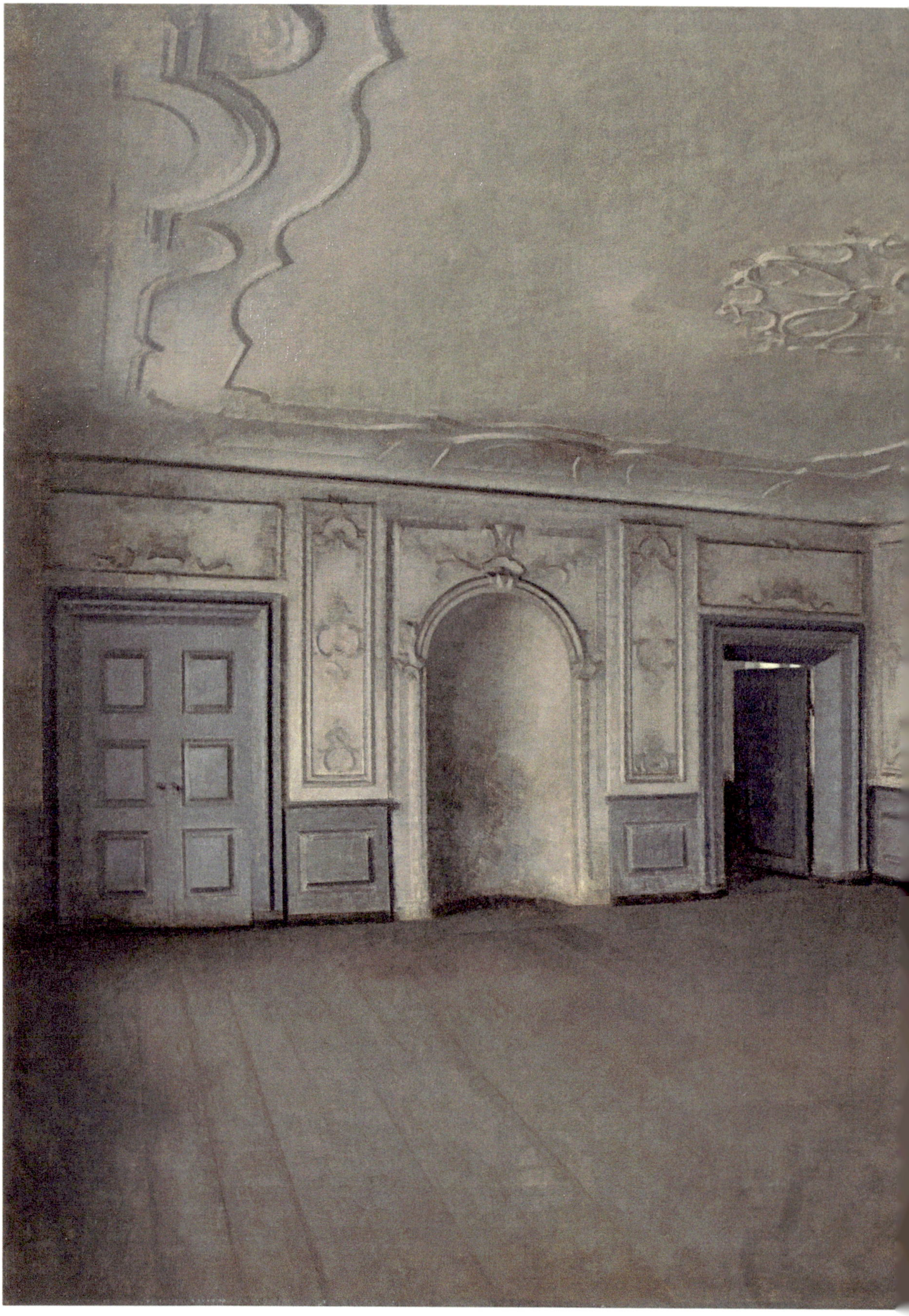

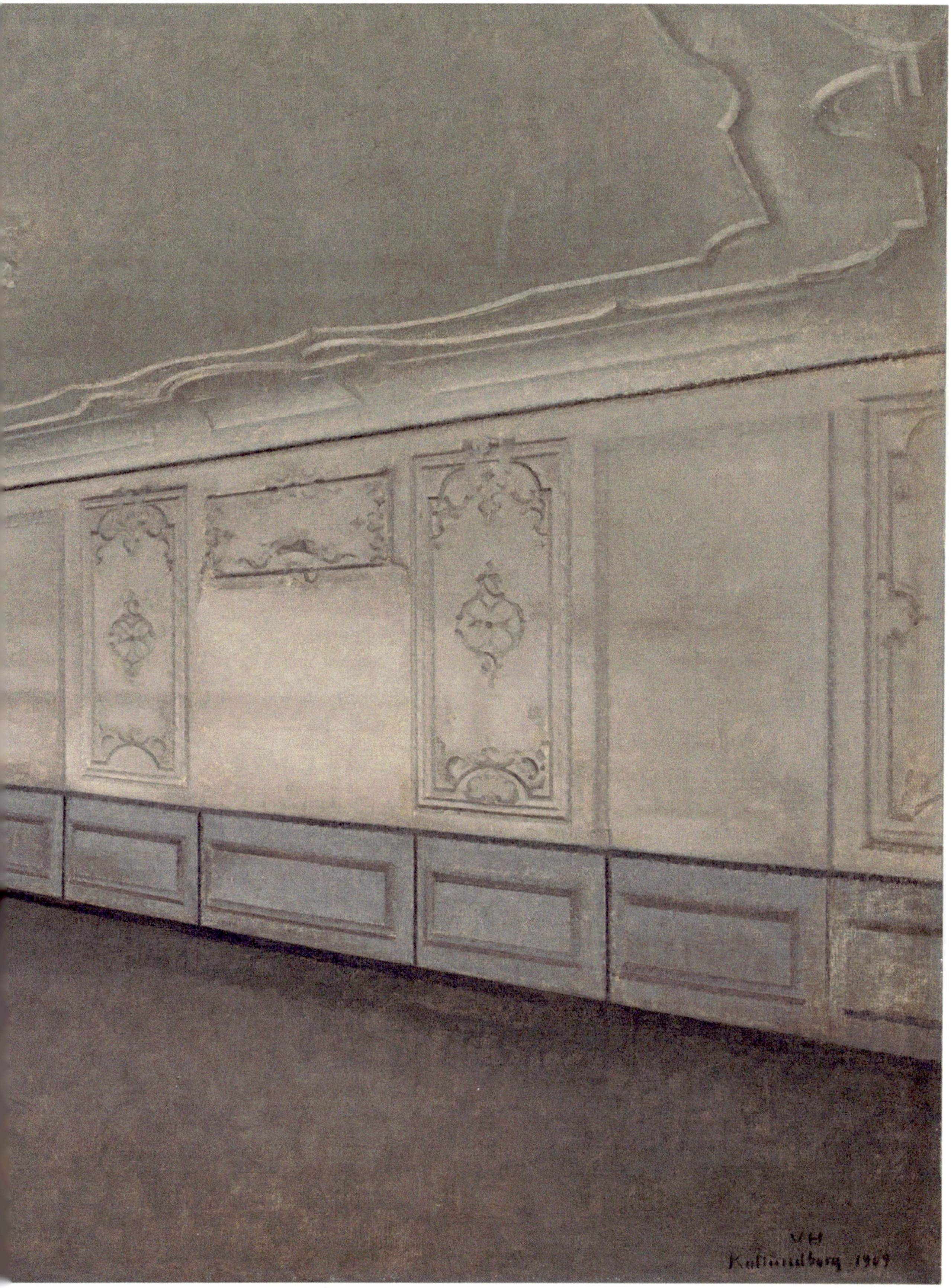
VH

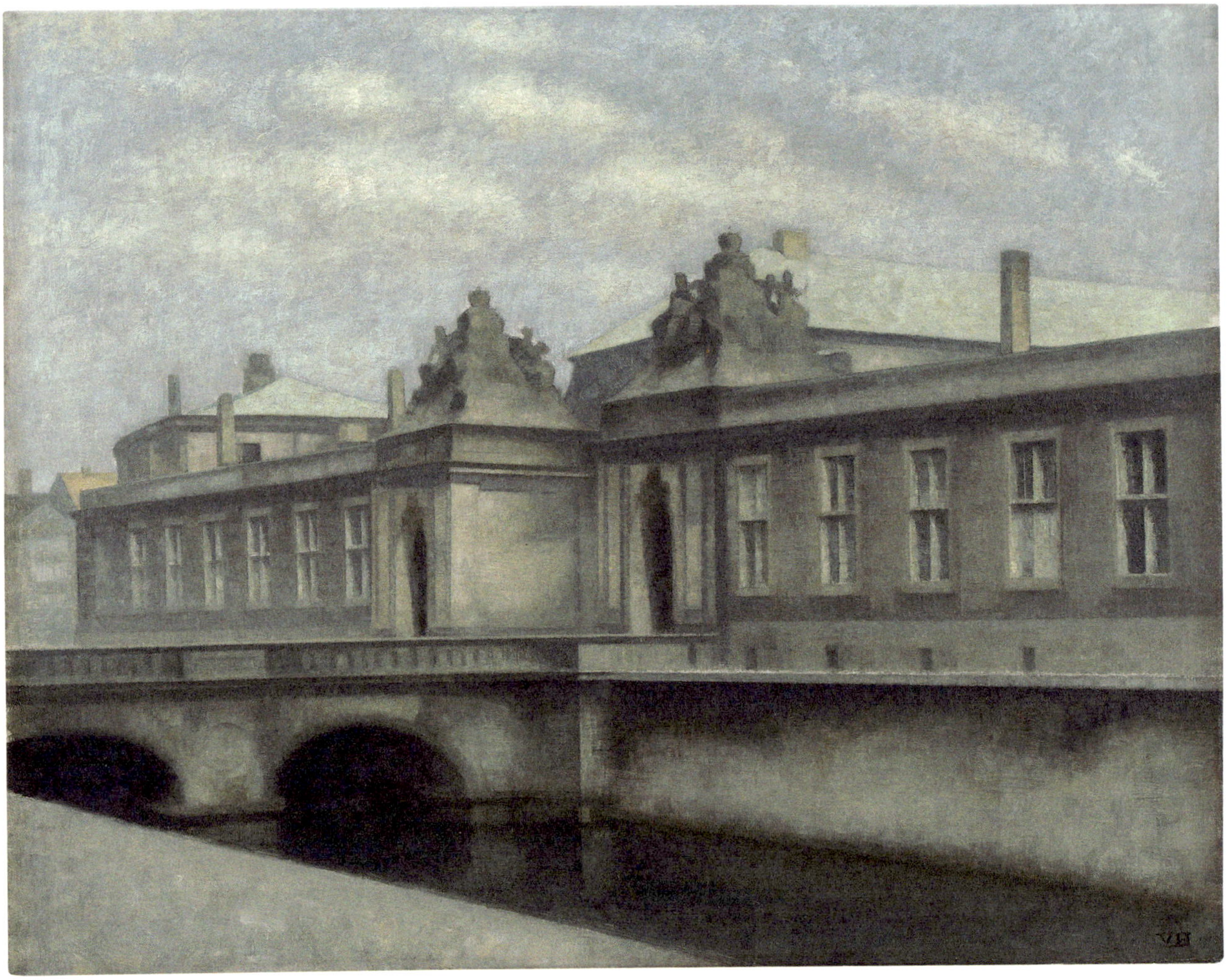

Christiansborg, 1914
Oil on canvas
20 ½ × 27 ⅛ inches (52 × 69 cm)

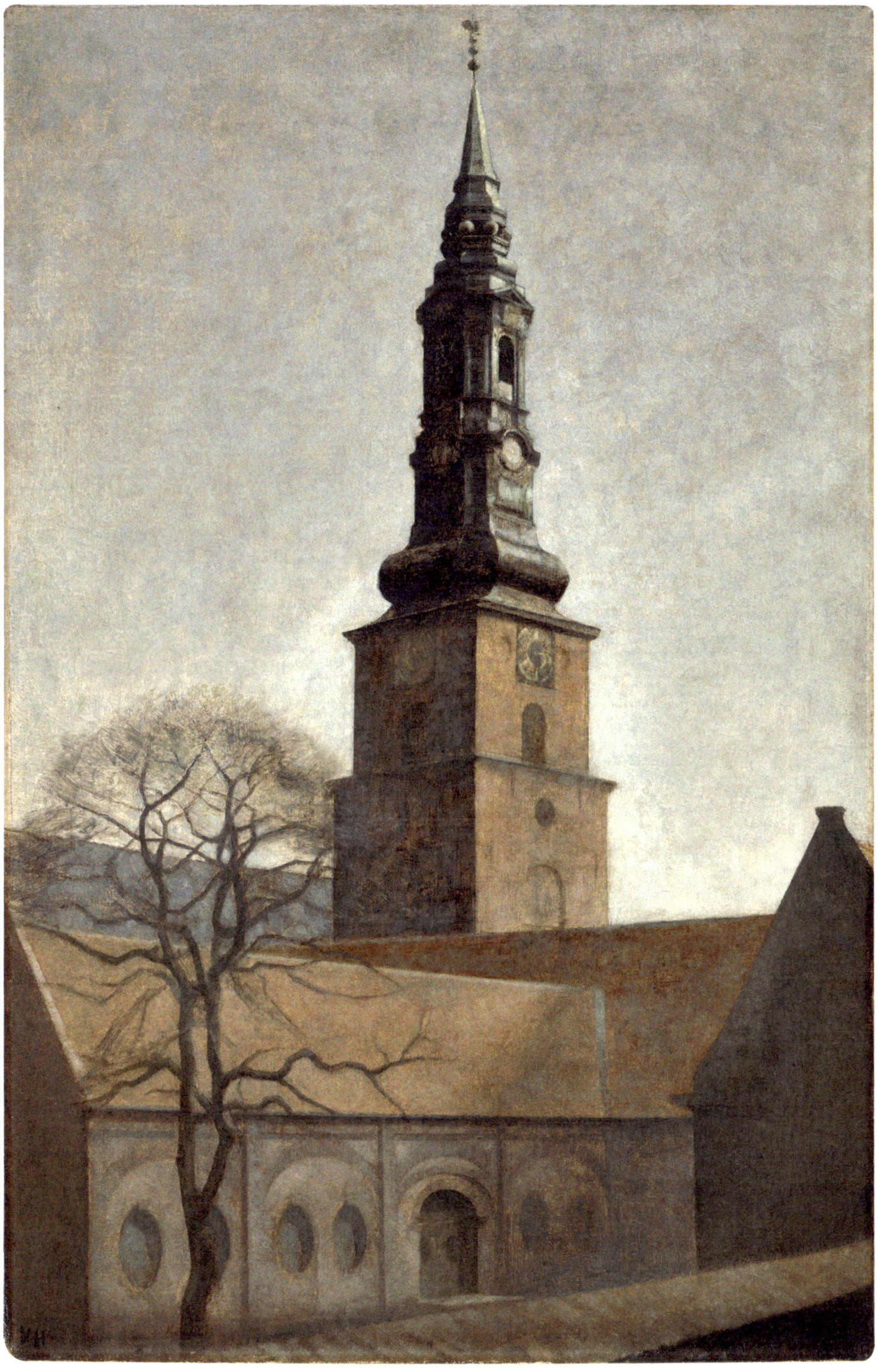

The Church of St. Peter, Copenhagen, ca. 1906
Oil on canvas
30 ½ × 20 ¼ inches (77.5 × 51.4 cm)

Morning Toilette, 1914
Oil on canvas
34 1/4 × 28 3/4 inches (87 × 73 cm)

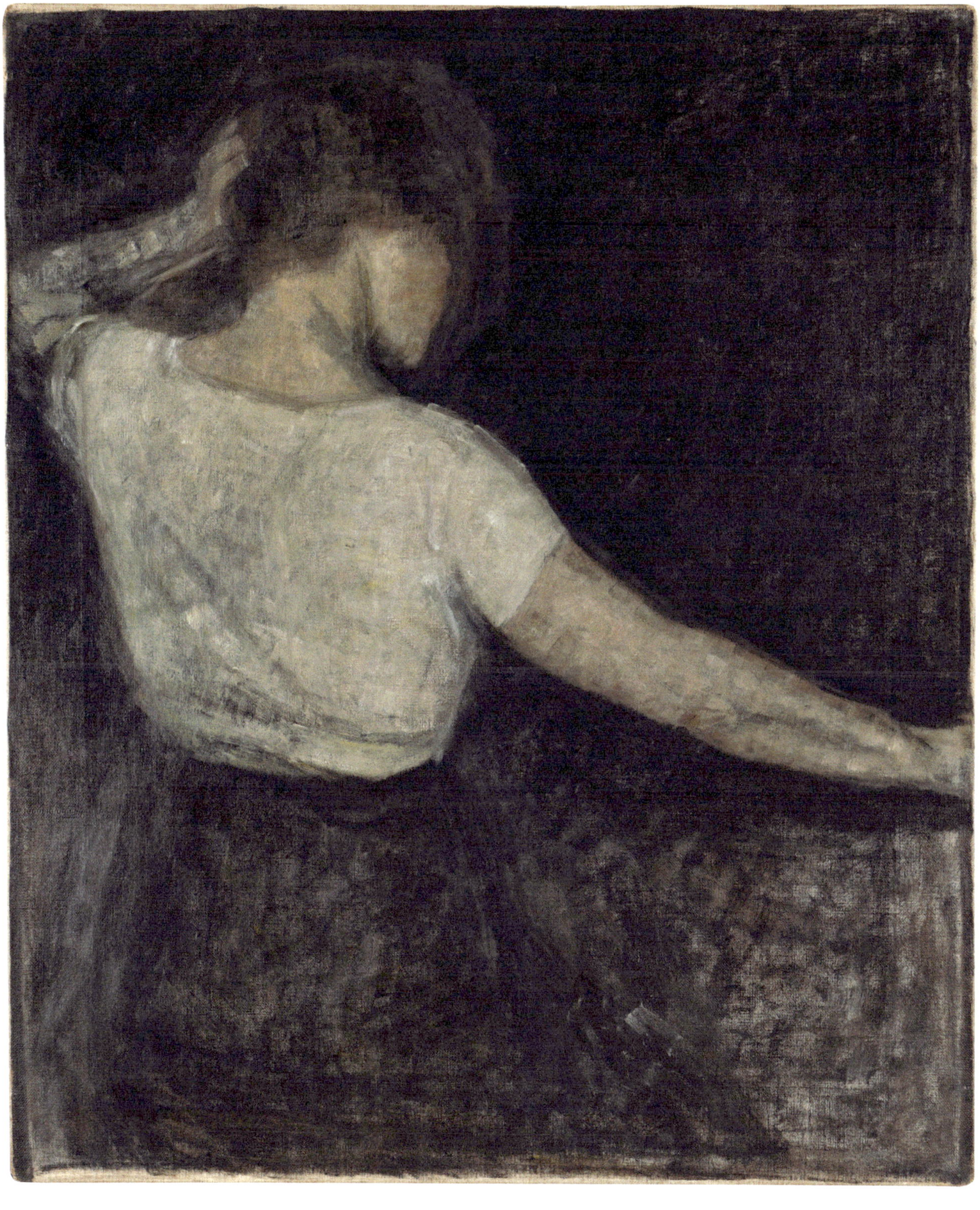

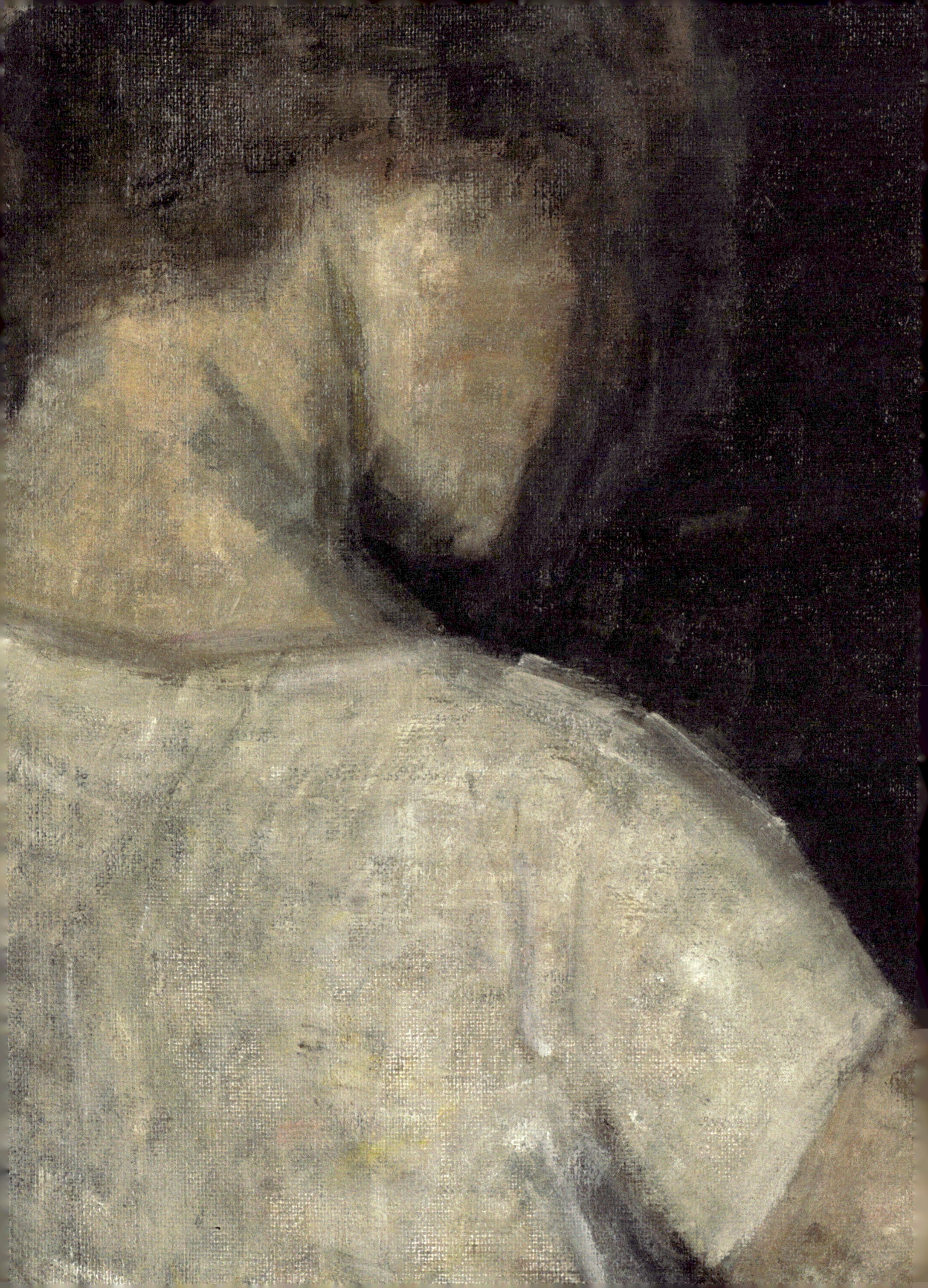

Interior with Windsor Chair, 1913
Oil on canvas
29 × 21½ inches (73.7 × 54.6 cm)

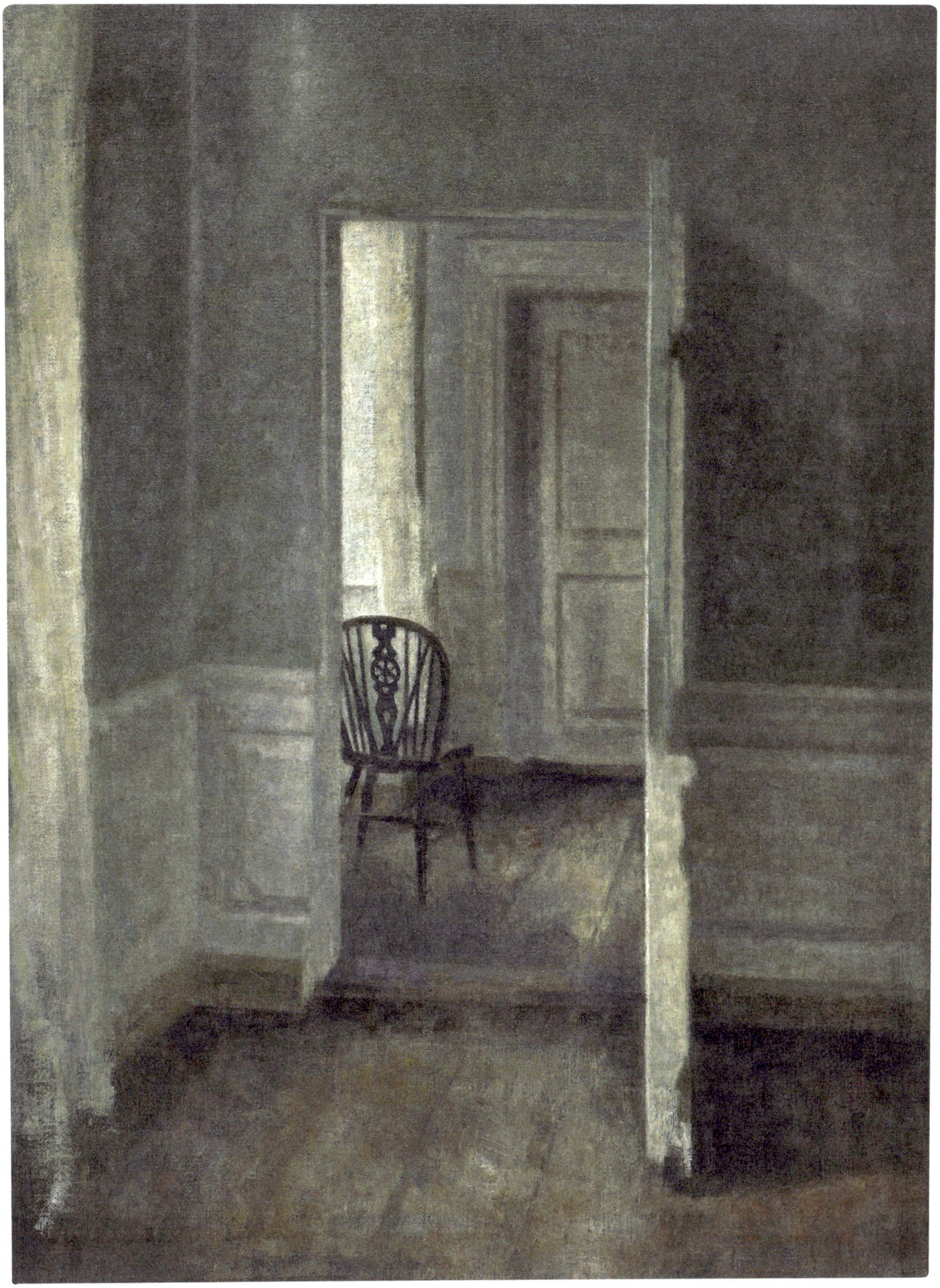

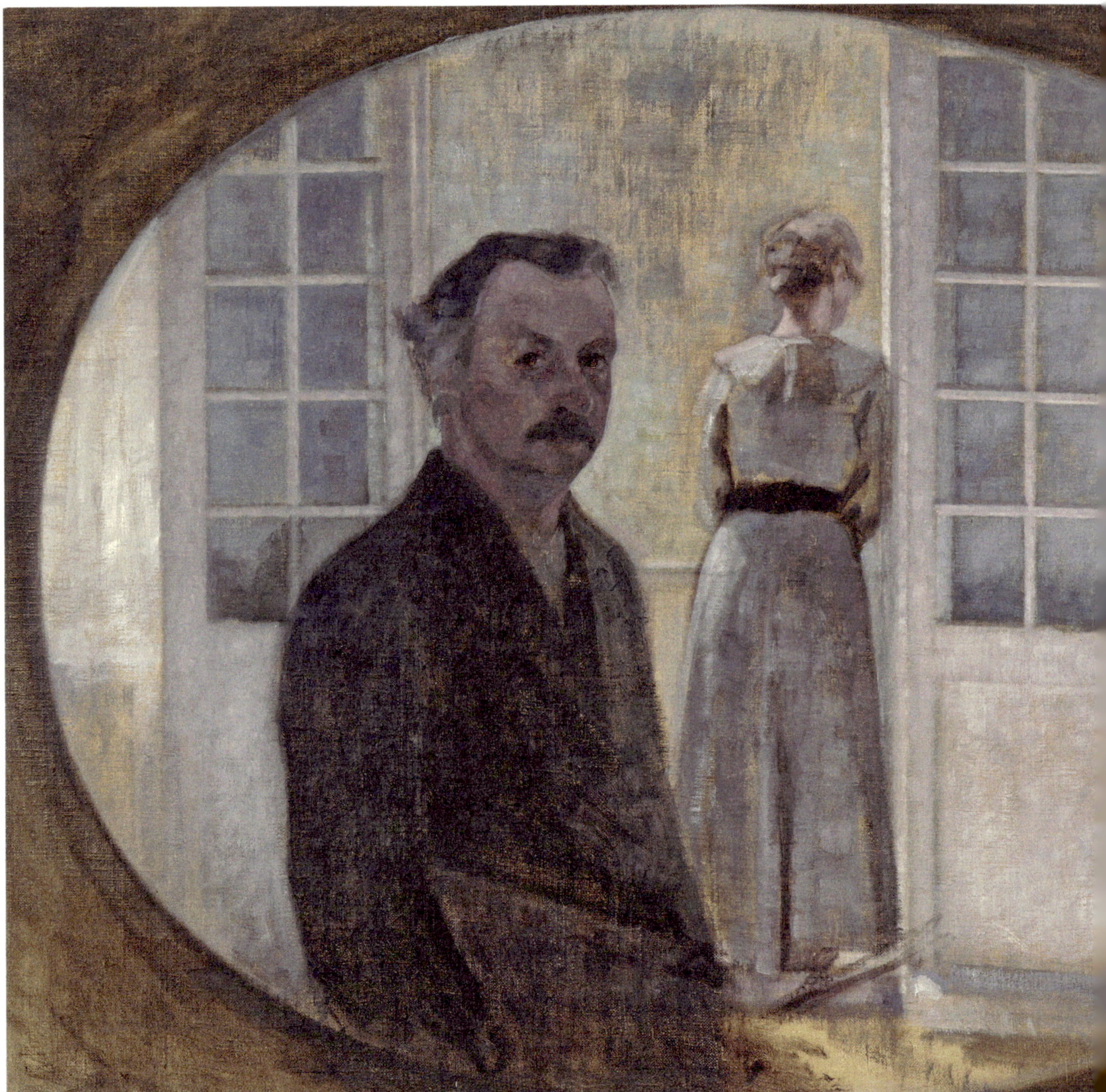

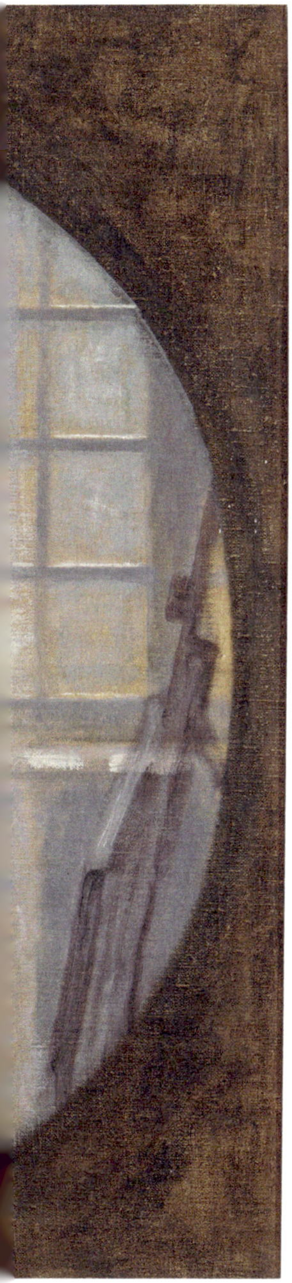

Double Portrait of the Artist and His Wife,
Seen through a Mirror. The Cottage Spurveskjul, 1911
Oil on canvas
21 5/8 × 29 7/8 inches (55 × 76 cm)

List of Works

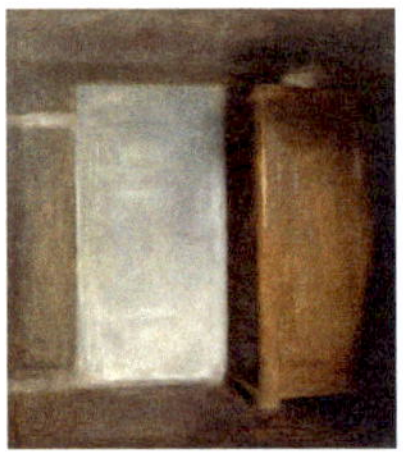

Interior with White Door and Yellow Wardrobe, 1886
Oil on canvas
15 3/8 × 14 3/8 inches (39 × 36.5 cm)
Private collection
p. 49

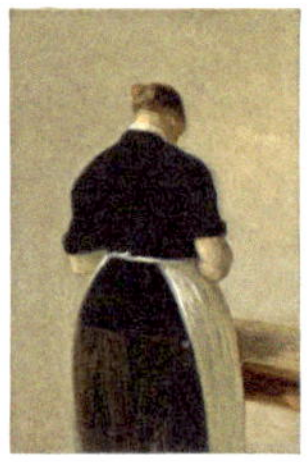

Study of Standing Woman, Seen from Behind, 1884–88
Oil on canvas
21 1/8 × 14 inches (53.7 × 35.6 cm)
Property from the Collection of Ambassador John L. Loeb Jr.
p. 50

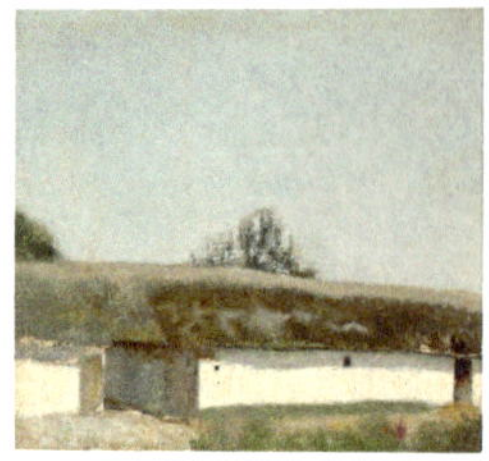

Landscape with a Barn, 1883
Oil on canvas
13 3/8 × 14 1/8 inches (34 × 36 cm)
Private collection
p. 52

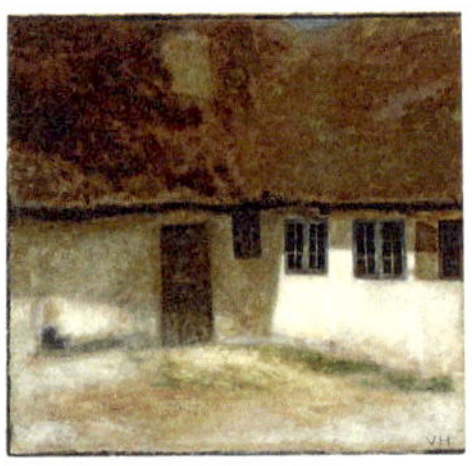

Farmhouse, 1883
Oil on canvas
13 3/8 × 14 1/8 inches (34 × 36 cm)
Private collection
p. 53

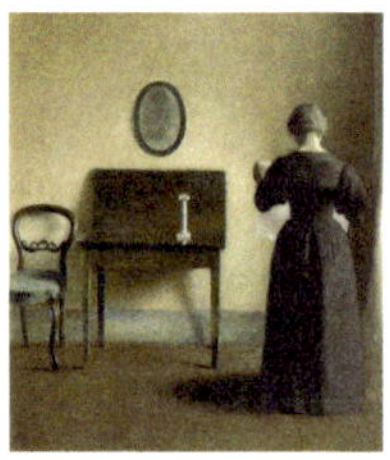

Interior with a Standing Woman, 1898
Oil on canvas
19 1/8 × 16 3/4 inches (48.5 × 42.4 cm)
Private collection
p. 55, detail pp. 56–57

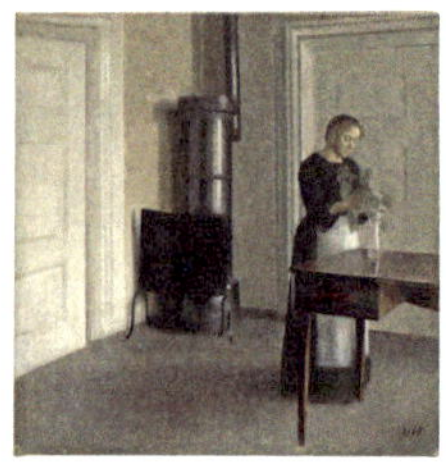

Interior with Woman Placing Branches in Vase on Table, 1900
Oil on canvas
15 7/8 × 15 1/2 inches (40.3 × 39.4 cm)
Property from the Collection of Ambassador John L. Loeb Jr.
p. 58

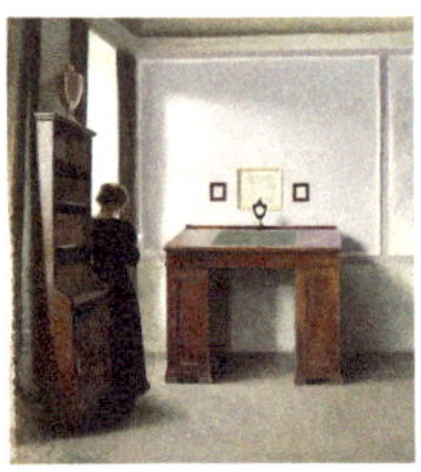

Interior with a Writing Desk, 1900
Oil on canvas
18 1/2 × 18 7/8 inches (47 × 48 cm)
Private collection
p. 61

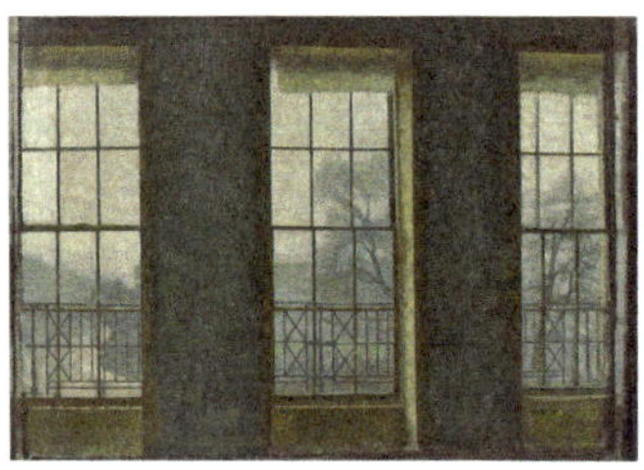

Interior in London, Brunswick Square, 1912
Oil on canvas
20 7/8 × 29 7/8 inches (53 × 76 cm)
Private collection
pp. 62–63

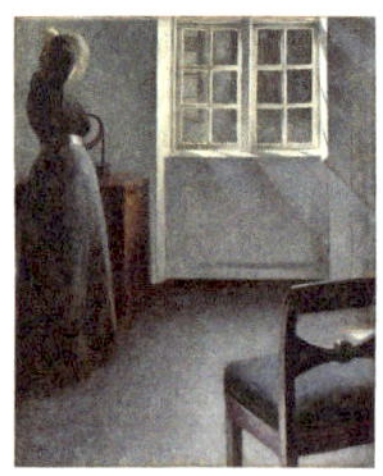

Woman before a Mirror, 1906
Oil on canvas
18 1/8 × 15 1/8 inches (46 × 38.5 cm)
Private collection
p. 65, detail pp. 66–67

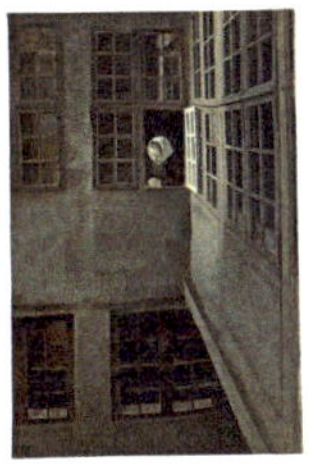

Courtyard Interior at Strandgade 30, ca. 1905
Oil on canvas, mounted on panel
32 × 21½ inches (81.3 × 54.6 cm)
Property from the Collection of
Ambassador John L. Loeb Jr.
p. 69

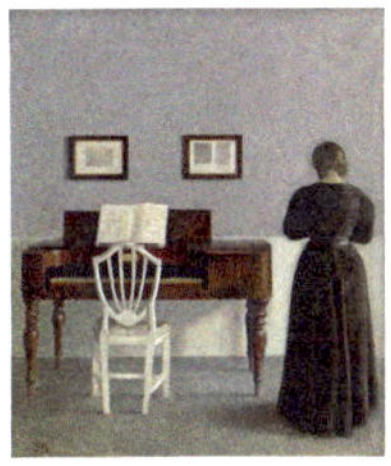

*Interior with the Artist's Wife,
Seen from Behind*, 1901
Oil on canvas
17¾ × 15⅜ inches (45 × 39 cm)
Private collection
p. 71

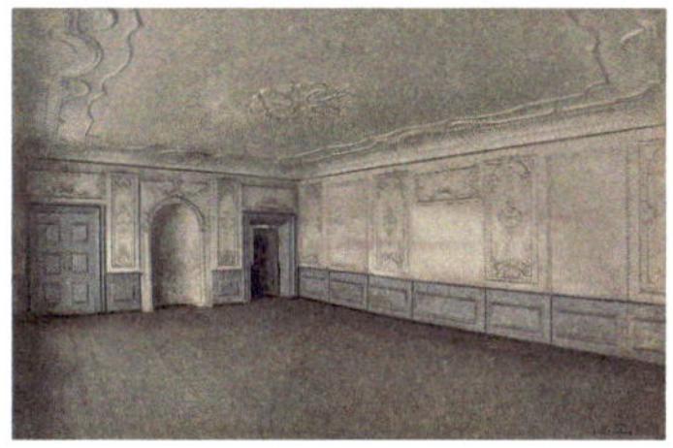

*Interior of the Great Hall
in Lindegaarden*, 1909
Oil on canvas
30⅜ × 46½ inches (77 × 118 cm)
Private collection
pp. 72–73

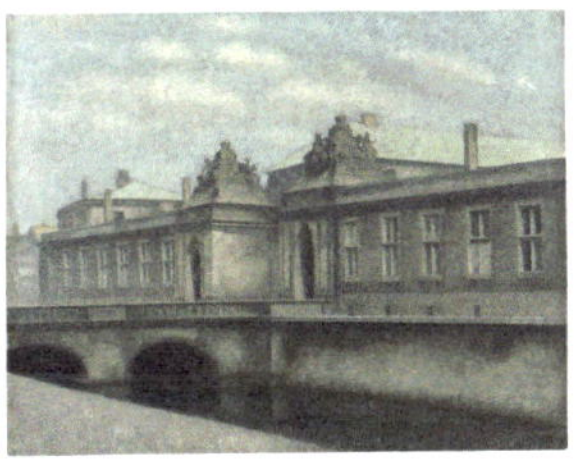

Christiansborg, 1914
Oil on canvas
20½ × 27⅛ inches (52 × 69 cm)
Private collection
p. 74

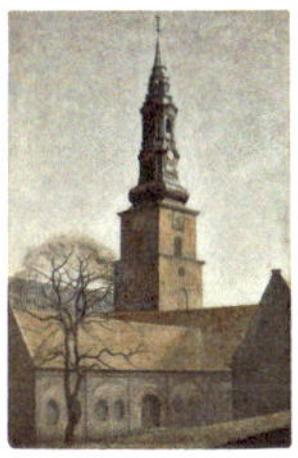

The Church of St. Peter, Copenhagen, ca. 1906
Oil on canvas
30½ × 20¼ inches (77.5 × 51.4 cm)
Property from the Collection of
Ambassador John L. Loeb Jr.
p. 75

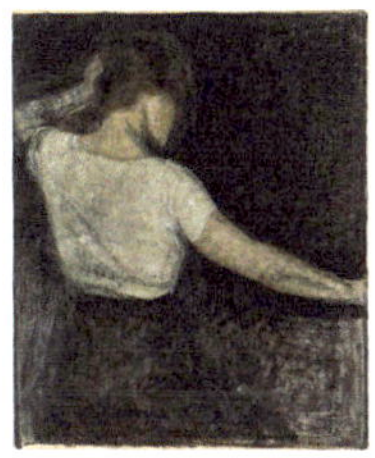

Morning Toilette, 1914
Oil on canvas
34¼ × 28¾ inches (87 × 73 cm)
Private collection
p. 77, detail pp. 78–79

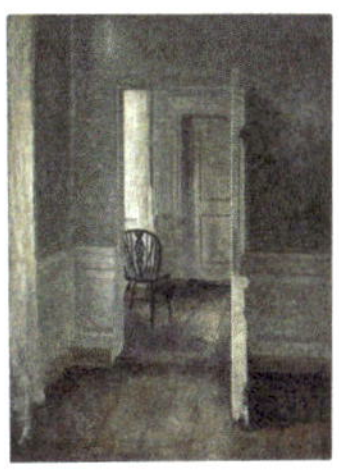

Interior with Windsor Chair, 1913
Oil on canvas
29 × 21½ inches (73.7 × 54.6 cm)
Property from the Collection of
Ambassador John L. Loeb Jr.
p. 81

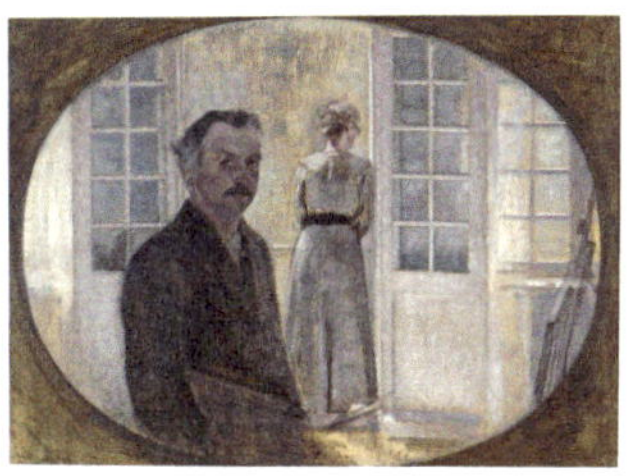

*Double Portrait of the Artist and His Wife,
Seen through a Mirror. The Cottage Spurveskjul*, 1911
Oil on canvas
21⅝ × 29⅞ inches (55 × 76 cm)
Private collection
pp. 82–83

Vilhelm Hammershøi: Stille

Felix Krämer

Der dänische Maler Vilhelm Hammershøi (1864–1916) redete wenig. Als der Künstler Emil Nolde ihn 1900 zuhause in Kopenhagen besuchte, notierte dieser anschliessend: «Er sprach langsam und leise, wir alle sprachen still.» Er sei «beharrlich schweigsam», sagten seine langjährigen Freunde. Aufgrund der zurückgezogenen Lebensweise verglichen sie den Maler mit einem Einsiedler und suchten nach medizinischen Erklärungen.

Hammershøi mied das gesellschaftliche Leben. Eröffnungen, Theaterpremieren und andere öffentliche Ereignisse waren für ihn ein Gräuel. So ist es vielleicht nicht überraschend, dass seine Biografie wenig spektakulär verlief. 1864 in Kopenhagen als Sohn eines Kaufmanns geboren, blieb er seiner Heimatstadt stets treu. Bereits früh erkannte Hammershøis Mutter das künstlerische Talent ihres zweitältesten Sohnes, das ab dem achten Lebensjahr durch privaten Zeichenunterricht gefördert wurde. Schon mit fünfzehn Jahren nahm er das Studium an der Königlichen Dänischen Kunstakademie in Kopenhagen auf. Hinzu kam die Ausbildung an der Freien Studienschule, die unzufriedene Studenten kurz zuvor aus Protest gegen die veralteten Lehrmethoden an der königlichen Akademie gegründet hatten. Hier gehörte Peder Severin Krøyer – damals ein internationaler Malerstar – zu seinen Lehrern. Krøyer wird die Aussage zugeschrieben, dass er seinen Schüler zwar nicht verstanden habe, diesen aber auch nicht beeinflussen wollte, da er sich bewusst gewesen wäre, dass hier ein aussergewöhnliches künstlerisches Werk entstünde.

Trotz seines zurückhaltenden Wesens stand Hammershøi gleich mehrfach im Zentrum von Kunstskandalen in Dänemark, die ihn schlagartig berühmt machten. Aus heutiger Perspektive kaum nachzuvollziehen, echauffierten sich die Akademieprofessoren und weite Teile der dänischen Öffentlichkeit 1885 über sein Ausstellungsdebüt *Porträt eines jungen Mädchens* (Abb. 1, S. 7). Mit der gedämpften Farbigkeit, dem unruhigen und leicht verschwommen wirkenden Pinselduktus sowie der unbestimmten Perspektivkonstruktion, die es dem Betrachter nicht leicht macht, einen festen Standpunkt zu beziehen, entsprach das Bild nicht den damaligen Erwartungen an ein Gemälde. Während ihn seine Kommilitonen dafür bewunderten, verweigerten die Professoren der Akademie ihre Anerkennung. Auch in den folgenden Jahren führten Hammershøis Bilder im konservativ geprägten Dänemark immer wieder zu Diskussionen.

Zu Hammershøis frühesten Gemälden zählen die beiden kleinformatigen Bauernhofdarstellungen aus dem Jahr 1883, die bereits wesentliche Charakteristika seiner Kunst aufweisen. In *Landschaft mit einer Scheune* verstellt der Stall die Sicht auf die Landschaft (S. 52). Wie eine Mauer reicht das Gebäude von einem bis zum anderen Bildrand. Von der Natur ist bis auf zwei Baumwipfel, die hinter dem

Dach hervorschauen und ein wenig Grün im Bildvordergrund, nichts zu sehen. Wie so oft bei Hammershøi ist der Himmel grau – weder Wind noch Vogel beleben die Szenerie. Still und starr erscheint die Welt. Die zunächst unscheinbare Darstellung verblüfft durch ihre Radikalität: Neben dem bewussten Verstellen-des-Blickes ist es vor allem der hohe Abstraktionsgrad, der für die damalige Zeit höchst ungewöhnlich ist.

Auch das Gemälde *Bauernhof* überrascht durch seine radikale Komposition (S. 53). Es zeigt ein Gebäude, dessen Dach und Fassade den grössten Teil des Bildfelds ausfüllen. Unklar bleibt, ob es sich dabei um einen Winkel des Hauses oder um eine flache Fassade handelt. Denn, während die Dachform – am oberen Bildrand ist ein kleines Stück Himmel zu erkennen – suggeriert, dass es sich um zwei separate Dächer handelt, wird dieser Eindruck durch die waagerecht durchlaufende Dachkante und die perspektivische Ausrichtung der Fenster gestört. In beiden Werken spielt Hammershøi mit der Erwartung des Betrachters, der nach eindeutigen Antworten sucht. Wie in einem Vexierbild, bleiben die Dinge in der Schwebe.

Ein weiteres Frühwerk, *Interieur mit weisser Tür und gelbem Schrank* (S. 49), bildet hier keine Ausnahme. Bei dem 1886 entstandenen Gemälde handelt es sich um Hammershøis erstes Interieur überhaupt. Auch hier sind bereits die wesentlichen Eigenschaften seines künstlerischen Œuvres vorhanden. Erneut ist die Komposition ungewöhnlich in ihrer rigiden, grafisch angelegten Struktur: Der Künstler konfrontiert den Betrachter frontal mit einer geschlossenen Tür. Diese ist, wie die gesamte Darstellung, allerdings so summarisch wiedergegeben, dass ihr nicht nur der Türgriff, sondern auch Zargen und selbst der Rahmen fehlen. Es sind vor allem die Proportionen und die Position auf der Wand, welche an eine Tür denken lassen. Während das Wandfeld links daneben leer ist, steht rechts neben der Tür ein grosser Schank, darauf ist eine helle Schale zu erkennen. Die Dimensionen des Möbelstücks lassen sich nur erahnen, da ein Schlagschatten seine Konturen in Dunkelheit hüllt und es zudem vom Bildrand abgeschnitten wird. Genau wie in den Bauernhofdarstellungen verzichtet Hammershøi in dem Interieur auf jegliches anekdotische Detail. Auch ist das Motiv denkbar banal. Hier gibt es nichts, was nach einer klassischen Kunstauffassung darstellungswürdig wäre, aber die Art und Weise, wie Hammershøi es darstellt, macht es aufregend.

Obwohl Hammershøi zurückgezogen in Kopenhagen lebte, begab er sich regelmässig auf Auslandsreisen in die europäischen Kunstzentren und war über die Kunst seiner Zeit gut informiert. Nach der Heirat mit Ida Ilsted, der Schwester seines Kommilitonen Peter Ilsted, verbrachte der Künstler 1891 ein halbes Jahr in Paris. Wichtiger als die Entwicklungen der zeitgenössischen Kunst war für ihn allerdings die holländische Genremalerei des 17. Jahrhunderts, deren Werke er zuvor in Holland und Belgien bewundert hatte. Neben Jan Vermeers geheimnisvollen Interieurs waren es Pieter de Hoochs, Emanuel de Wittes und Pieter Janssens Elingas Stubenbilder, die ihn faszinierten. Er war damit keineswegs allein: Diese Bilder erfreuten sich schon damals bei Kunstliebhabern grosser Popularität und wurden als Spiegelbilder eines wohlgeordneten Alltags interpretiert, als Visionen privaten Glücks.

Eine wichtige Rolle spielte für Hammershøi London, das er insgesamt fünf Mal besuchte. Neben seiner Heimatstadt verbrachte er an keinem anderen Ort mehr Zeit. Hier malte der Künstler 1898 auch das *Interieur mit einer stehenden Frau* (S. 55). Das Bild ist eng verwandt mit einem gleichzeitig entstandenen Gemälde, das sich heute in der Sammlung des Nationalmuseums in Stockholm befindet (Abb. 2, S. 9). Während dieses Werk Ida stehend hinter einem mit weissem Tuch gedeckten Tisch zeigt, fehlt dieses Möbelstück in der zweiten Variante. Hier steht Ida, erneut den Rücken zum Betrachter gewandt, frei im Raum. In beiden Bildern ist ein halb hochgeklappter Tisch vor der Wand platziert, darüber hängt jeweils ein ovaler Spiegel: Obwohl der Betrachter frontal in den Spiegel blickt, ist kein Abbild zu sehen, zu erkennen ist lediglich eine graue Fläche. Der Maler hat in der Stockholmer Variante auf dem Klapptisch eine Topfpflanze platziert, in dem anderen Bild einen leeren weissen Kerzenleuchter. Ob Ida eine Zeitung liest oder eine weisse Tischdecke in der Hand hält, bleibt offen.

Wenngleich Hammershøi vor allem für Interieur-Darstellungen wie diese bekannt ist, standen bis zu seiner Rückkehr aus London die Gattungen Porträt, Landschafts- und Architekturdarstellungen gleichberechtigt in seinem Œuvre nebeneinander. Erst der unmittelbar nach der Rückkehr nach Kopenhagen erfolgte Einzug in die Strandgade 30 änderte dies. Bis heute existiert im Stadtteil Christianshavn das Backsteingebäude aus dem 17. Jahrhundert, in dem der Künstler zwischen 1898 und 1909 lebte (Abb. 3,4, S. 10–11). Und auch den Innenhof des Gebäudes mit seinen zahlreichen Fenstern, den er ca. 1905 malte, gibt es noch (S. 69). Die Wohnung in der ersten Etage war nicht nur sein Zuhause und sein Atelier, sie wurde vor allem zu seinem wichtigsten Motiv. Eingerichtet waren die Zimmer mit wenigen historischen Möbeln und Objekten; Gegenstände, die sich in Hammershøis Bildern immer wieder finden. Weder die sparsame Möblierung noch die Schlichtheit der Einrichtungsgegenstände entsprachen dem damals herrschenden Zeitgeschmack, der reich verzierte und opulent ausgestattete Räume bevorzugte.

Ein gutes Beispiel für Hammershøis in der Strandgade 30 entstandene Interieur-Darstellungen sind vier Bilder, die er zwischen 1900 und 1906 malte. Die beiden frühesten, jeweils zwei Jahre nach dem Einzug geschaffenen Werke, zeigen Ida in den zur Straße gelegenen Räumen. Während das Gemälde *Interieur mit Frau Zweige in eine Vase auf einen Tisch stellend* (S. 58) für das Œuvre des Künstlers ungewöhnlich zugänglich ist, da man Ida nicht nur von vorne sieht, sondern auch ihre Tätigkeit deutlich erkennen kann, entspricht *Interieur mit einem Schreibpult* Hammershøis Vorliebe, den Betrachter im Unklaren zu lassen. Es zeigt Ida an einem Fenster stehend, dem Betrachter den Rücken zugekehrt, halb verdeckt von einem Bücherschrank (S. 61). Vermutlich liest sie im hereinströmenden Tageslicht einen Brief: Doch weder der Inhalt des Schreibens noch ihre Reaktion darauf, lässt sich deuten. Ein wuchtiges Schreibpult beansprucht den meisten Platz innerhalb der Bildkomposition: Es ist leicht aus der Mittelachse verschoben, frontal vor der Wand platziert. Eine kleine darauf stehende Vase sowie drei an der Wand hängende Bilder lenken den Blick noch zusätzlich darauf. Im Verhältnis zu dem Möbel ist Ida auffällig klein, wodurch dieses noch massiger wirkt. Auch die Aufteilung der Objekte im Raum irritiert: während die rechte Bildseite leer bleibt, befinden sich alle genannten Darstellungselemente auf der linken Seite. So entsteht ein Spannungsverhältnis, das die zunächst so harmonisch erscheinende Komposition prägt. Mit diesen kompositorischen Entscheidungen untergräbt Hammershøi die konventionelle Hierarchie, denn anders als erwartet, ist es nicht Ida, die die Szene beherrscht, sondern das Schreibpult.

Zahlreiche Interieur-Darstellungen – wie das im Jahr 1901 gemalte Werk *Interieur mit der Frau des Künstlers in Rückansicht* (S. 71) – zeigen Ida im dunklen bodenlangen Kleid als Rückenfigur. Sie steht neben einem Hammerklavier, ihre Arme angewinkelt, den Kopf leicht geneigt. Erneut bleibt Idas Tätigkeit unklar. Am Klavier ist ein weisser Stuhl platziert, dahinter auf dem Instrument ein aufgeschlagenes Notenheft. An der Wand hängen zwei Bilder. Das weisse Passepartout deutet an, dass es sich um Grafiken handelt. Die Motive sind nicht zu erkennen. Sämtliche hier dargestellten Objekte sind aus dem Hammershøi-Kosmos wohl bekannt und kommen in zahlreichen seiner Bilder vor. Auch wenn der Künstler immer real existierende Gegenstände malte, wäre es naiv zu glauben, dass er permanent die Wohnung umgeräumt und neugestaltet hätte.

Zu Hammershøis ungewöhnlichsten Werken gehört das ebenfalls in der Strandgade 30 entstandene Werk *Frau vor dem Spiegel* von 1906 (S. 65). Während die beiden gerade vorgestellten Interieurs das zur Strasse gelegene Wohnzimmer zeigen, sind wir nun in einem der hinteren zum Innenhof ausgerichteten Räume. Zu sehen ist das Fenster, das aus *Tanz der Staubkörner* (1900) – vermutlich Hammershøis populärstem Gemälde – vertraut ist (Abb. 5, S. 13). Ida, ganz links im Bild, scheint gerade vor einem kleinen auf einer Kommode stehenden Spiegel ihre Frisur zu richten. Sie steht leicht seitlich gedreht und wirkt weniger statisch als üblich. Durch den erhobenen Arm ist ihr Gesicht auch hier nicht zu sehen. Vorne links am Bildrand ist ein Stuhl platziert, als wäre ein Betrachter anwesend, der die Szene mustert. Wie in kaum einer anderen Darstellung Hammershøis finden sich hier das durch das Fenster strömende Sonnenlicht, Bewegung und Raum zu einem vielschichtigen, eng verwobenen Ganzen zusammen.

Auch nach seinem Auszug aus der Strandgade 30 – das Haus war damals in einem so baufälligen Zustand, dass es einzustürzen drohte – malte er weiter die privaten Räume seiner Wohnungen. Neben Gemälden entstanden auch einige Zeichnungen. Bei dem vorliegenden Blatt (S. 23) handelt es sich um die zeichnerische Fassung eines Gemäldes von 1910 (Abb. 6, S. 15). Welches der beiden Werke zuerst entstand, lässt sich nicht mit Gewissheit sagen. Die Arbeiten zeigen das geräumige Wohn- und Musikzimmer der Wohnung in der Bredgade 25, in der der Künstler ab 1910 drei Jahre lebte. Ebenfalls in dieser Zeit malte Hammershøi ein Selbstporträt, das ihn gemeinsam mit seiner Frau zeigt (S. 82–83). Während der Künstler an der Staffelei steht und den Betrachter direkt ansieht, verharrt Ida im Hintergrund als Rückenfigur im weissen Kleid. Umschlossen wird das gesamte Interieur von einer elliptischen Rahmenform, die deutlich macht, dass die Welt des Künstlers und die des Betrachters zwei getrennte Sphären sind.

Zu Hammershøis kompromisslosesten Werken zählen Das *Interieur der grossen Halle im Lindegaarden* von 1909 und *Interieur in London, Brunswick Square*, das er 1912 bei seinem letzten Besuch in England malte (S. 72–73 und 62–63). Beide Bilder konfrontieren den Betrachter mit menschenleeren Raumansichten: Das 1909 entstandene Gemälde gibt, wie durch eine Weitwinkellinse gesehen, einen grossen leergeräumten Festsaal wieder, dessen verspielte Wand und Deckenpanelen den Künstler offensichtlich in ihren Bann zogen. In dem drei Jahre später gemalten Werk zeigt der Maler den Blick auf die Fensterfront seines Londoner Apartments. Anders als es bei dem Motiv eines Fensterbildes zu erwarten wäre, lässt Hammershøi den Betrachter nicht wirklich am Ausblick teilhaben. Nur schemenhaft zeichnen sich im Dunst eine Strasse mit Gebäuden sowie einige spärlich belaubte Bäume ab. Wie wichtig dem Künstler dieses Gemälde war, belegen Fotografien aus seiner Wohnung in Kopenhagen – wo es in seinem Schlafzimmer hing.

Hammershøis Interieurs sind eine Genremalerei, der das Erzählerische fehlt, die nichts über die Bewohner verrät. Obwohl der Künstler den Betrachter immer wieder zu sich nach Hause einlädt, teilt er nichts Privates. Es ist eine grosse Stille, die Hammerhøis Räume beherrscht und deren Präsenz den Betrachter in ihren Bann zieht. Verstärkt wird dieser Effekt durch die auf wenige gedämpfte Farben konzentrierte Palette, die keine Ablenkung bietet. «Sie können vielleicht am besten als neutrale und reduzierte Farben bezeichnet werden. Ich bin zutiefst überzeugt, dass ein Bild den besten Effekt hat im farblichen Sinne, je weniger Farben es hat», so fasste der Künstler 1907 in einem seiner raren Interviews die besondere Wirkung seiner Farben zusammen. Seine Gemälde setzen sich aus einer Vielzahl von Farbschichten zusammen. Gewöhnlich arbeitete der Künstler lange an einem Bild und nuancierte erst im Laufe des Malprozesses die einzelnen Farb- und Schattenwirkungen. Mit kurzen, breit gesetzten Pinselstrichen trug er die recht trockene Ölfarbe auf die Leinwand auf. Gut nachvollziehen lässt sich dieses Vorgehen in seinem Gemälde *Morgentoilette* von 1914 (S. 77). Nicht nur in seiner rohen und offenen Ausführung erinnert das Bild – von dem eine weitere Fassung existiert – an seine wenige Jahre zuvor entstandenen Aktdarstellungen (Abb. 7, S. 18), in denen der Künstler das Gesicht seiner Frau durch Übermalung unkenntlich machte. Auch hier erzeugt diese Auslöschung des Gesichts ein Gefühl der Distanz, die in einem merkwürdigen Widerspruch zu dem Motiv steht.

Hammershøis Stadtansichten entsprechen ebenfalls kaum der Darstellungspraxis seiner Zeit, welche die Stadt als lebendigen Ort ständiger Bewegung schildert. Seine urbanen Szenen wirken merkwürdig leblos und distanziert. Zeichen städtischer Lebendigkeit wie Passanten, Fuhrwerke, trocknende Wäsche oder rauchende Schornsteine sucht man vergeblich. Dieses gilt auch für die Bilder, die das Zentrum seiner Heimatstadt Kopenhagen zeigen. Schon Zeitgenossen fühlten sich angesichts der Leere und der melancholischen Grundstimmung dieser Bilder an verlassene Städte erinnert.

Das Gemälde *Christiansborg*, das Hammershøi 1914, zwei Jahre vor seinem Tod malte und das zu seinen letzten Bildern zählt, ist beispielhaft für diese Arbeiten (S. 74). Es gehört zu einer Gruppe von Darstellungen des Schlosses, die den im Herzen Kopenhagens gelegenen Bau aus unterschiedlichen Perspektiven zeigt. Seit 1890 malte der Künstler in unregelmässigen Abständen immer wieder das Gebäude. In keinem der Bilder erkennt man, dass das Hauptgebäude des Schlosses bis auf seine Grundmauern abgebrannt war und es sich um eine Baustelle handelte. Dass der Wiederaufbau lange und kontrovers diskutiert wurde, letzte Arbeiten konnten erst 1937 abgeschlossen werden, war den zeitgenössischen Betrachtern genauso bewusst, wie die tragische Geschichte des Bauwerks selbst. In dem ausgestellten Gemälde rückt Hammershøi die Hofgebäude und die über den Frederiksholms Kanal führende sogenannte Marmorbrücke ins Zentrum; sie hatten das Feuer überstanden. Durch den tief angesetzten Blickpunkt ist von dem neu errichteten Hauptgebäude des Schlosses nichts zu sehen. Auch führt die Perspektive dazu, dass die Architektur noch abweisender und verschlossener erscheint. Gleiches trifft auf das Wasser des Kanals zu: Kaum vorstellbar, dass hier Leben möglich ist.

Diese Atmosphäre des Unbewohnbaren gilt auch für Hammershøis Landschaftsdarstellungen. Stets malte er gut erschlossene Gegenden, ohne jedoch Menschen oder Tiere abzubilden. Bei *Landschaft, Gentofte* von 1903 sind eine vielbefahrene Allee und ein Bauernhof ausserhalb von Kopenhagen zu sehen (Abb. 8, S. 20). Bemerkenswert an der Darstellung ist allerdings die Dominanz von der im Vordergrund befindlichen Wasserfläche und des Himmels – zwischen die sich die Landschaft als schmaler Streifen schiebt. Offensichtlich ist auch hier, dass der Künstler, anders als viele seiner Zeitgenossen, keine romantische Sehnsucht nach unberührter Natur suggeriert. Hammershøi ist vielmehr von der grafischen Struktur des Motivs fasziniert. Der Vorstellung einer ungezügelten Natur begegnet der Künstler durch die Strenge seiner Komposition und die Nüchternheit seiner Malerei.

Ein Blick in die zeitgenössischen Rezensionen hilft – wie so oft –, um Hammershøis Kunst besser zu verstehen. Um 1900 verglichen ihn Kritiker mit so unterschiedlichen Künstlern wie James McNeill Whistler, Edvard Munch und Max Klinger: Obwohl das Werk dieser Maler sehr verschieden ist, sah man in ihren und auch Hammershøis Arbeiten einen Beitrag zum Symbolismus. Dieser zeichnete sich nicht durch eine gemeinsame stilistische Eigenart, sondern vielmehr durch eine verwandte Geisteshaltung aus, die hinter der sichtbaren Oberfläche die Essenz des Lebens zu erkennen glaubte. Zudem wurde Hammershøis Malerei wiederholt mit den Werken der symbolistischen Schriftsteller Maurice Maeterlinck und George Rodenbach in Verbindung gebracht, die in der Stille und Zurückgezogenheit innere Erfüllung suchten. Maeterlinck schreibt in seinem Essay *Das Schweigen*: «Wir sprechen nur in den Stunden, wo wir nicht leben [...]. Und sobald wir sprechen, sagt uns etwas im Innern, dass göttliche Türen irgendwo schliessen.» Die Sprachlosigkeit wird damit zur Idealform menschlicher Kommunikation stilisiert, die zu grundlegenden Einsichten führe.

Dass schon Mitte des 19. Jahrhunderts der dänische Philosoph Søren Kierkegaard die Stille als idealen Zustand für die Suche nach Authentizität und tieferen Erkenntnissen ansah, ist mit Blick auf Hammershøi sicherlich kein Zufall. Zu dessen Lebzeiten wurde der Philosoph als einer der wichtigsten Denker Dänemarks bewundert. Hammershøi, der über eine umfangreiche Bibliothek verfügte, besass allein von Kierkegaard sieben Bücher, darunter mehrere Erstausgaben. Auch Kierkegaards bekanntestes Werk *Entweder – Oder* (1843) gehörte dazu.

Obwohl Hammershøis Malerei bereits zu Beginn seiner Karriere auch international wahrgenommen wurde, geriet es nach seinem Tod 1916 zunehmend in Vergessenheit. Zu sehr widersprach die stille, puristische Malerei den ruhelosen Experimenten der Nachkriegsavantgarde. Erst die Wiederentdeckung des Symbolismus seit den 1970er-Jahren und damit einhergehend die Neubewertung der figurativen Malerei als wichtigen Beitrag zur Kunst der Gegenwart hat Hammershøis von rätselhafter Schwermut durchdrungene Bilder in den Fokus gerückt. Galt der Künstler vielen seiner Zeitgenossen als eigenbrötlerischer Sonderling, wird er heute als Seelenverwandter von Jan Vermeer und Edward Hopper bewundert. Keinem anderen Maler des späten 19. Jahrhunderts war in den letzten Jahrzehnten ein so rasanter Aufstieg vergönnt: vom Geheimtipp zum Publikumsliebling. Vielbeachtete Retrospektiven in Paris, New York, London und Tokio haben die besondere Faszination seiner Kunst einem grossen Publikum vor Augen geführt. Anders als noch vor wenigen Jahren ist Hammershøi mittlerweile in den wichtigsten Museumssammlungen auch ausserhalb Skandinaviens prominent vertreten. Gleichzeitig begeistert sein Werk viele Künstler der Gegenwart, wie die Ausstellung *There I Belong. Hammershøi by Elmgreen und Dragset* 2019 im Statens Museums for Kunst in Kopenhagen belegt. Die von Michael Elmgreen und Ingar Dragset kuratierte Schau zeigte Hammershøis Interieurs Seite an Seite mit Werken der beiden Künstler-Kuratoren und Arbeiten zahlreicher Kolleginnen und Kollegen, darunter Monica Bonvicini, Ugo Rondinone und Thomas Ruff. Es ist offensichtlich, dass Hammershøi mit seiner Malerei den Nerv heutiger Generationen trifft. Seine Kunst erscheint wie ein Gegenentwurf zu der lauten und hektischen Welt, in der wir leben. Innehalten, schweigen, Stille zulassen: Diese Sehnsucht nach Ruhe und Entschleunigung erfährt durch Hammershøis Malerei ihre künstlerische Gestalt.

Erinnerungen an die Zukunft

Bei Vilhelm Hammershøi
berühren sich Zeit und Ewigkeit

Florian Illies

Was macht Vilhelm Hammershøi zu einem solch eminent zeitgenössischen Künstler? Er war nur Gast in seiner Zeit um 1900: Wie ein Abgesandter aus der Zukunft hat er in seinen Bildern seine Gegenwart immer bereits als eine Vergangenheit erinnert. Ja, seine Bilder speisen sich aus Erfahrungen der Moderne, also des 20. und des 21. Jahrhunderts, die sie eigentlich noch gar nicht gemacht haben können. Genau dieses geheime Wissen aus einer Zeit, die erst lange nach Hammershøis Tod beginnen wird, macht seine Bilder zu so notwendigen Bestandteilen unserer verunsicherten Gegenwart. Hammershøi wachte auf in einer Zeit, in der er «keine Ursache» hatte, wie sein Bewunderer Rainer Maria Rilke es nannte, wenn Künstler aus ihrer Zeit herausfallen. Aus ihm sprach schon Zukünftiges. Er erahnte schon vor über hundert Jahren genau jene Räume, in die unsere Seelen jetzt einziehen wollen.

•

Das Neue. Was Hammershøi im ausgehenden 19., beginnenden 20. Jahrhundert malte, war grundlegend neu. Ja, er war viel gereist durch ganz Europa, er hatte gesehen, was James McNeill Whistler in England an neuartigen Bilderscheinungen schuf und was Eugène Carrière und Pierre Puvis de Chavannes in Paris erdachten. Dennoch baute er aus der Kenntnis dieser Meister des Dunstes und der Uneindeutigkeit ein Œeuvre von grösster Eigenständigkeit.

Das wirklich *Neue* in der Kunst hat eine einzigartige Qualität: Es ist neu in seiner jeweiligen Zeit, zugleich aber konserviert es dieses *Neue* in sich als unzerstörbare Qualität für alle Zeiten. Die Neuartigkeit eines Giotto, eines Leonardo, eines Caravaggio, eines Goya, eines Manet, eines Picasso, eines Warhol – sie spricht genauso zu uns wie sie schon zu ihren Zeitgenossen sprach. Und natürlich entzündet sich das neue *Neue* immer nur an dem anderen, späteren oder früheren *Neuem*. Es ist eine geheime Formel für ein ewiges Leben, die dieser besonderen Malerei eingeschrieben ist, und die sie problemlos mit den Erneuerern aus anderen Zeiten und Räumen verbindet.

•

Gegen die Beschleunigung. Das ist das grosse Thema der Moderne, ihr geheimer Motor, ihre grösste Kraft: die Beschleunigung. Man kann das 20. Jahrhundert nicht ohne sie denken. Gerade in der Zeit um 1900 reisst sie alles mit sich: die Menschen, die Emotionen, die Gewissheiten, die Ideologien, die Staaten. Und am Ende auch die Utopien. Es geht um den Aufbruch in eine neue Zeit, um den Aufbruch in eine neue Psychologie, eine neue

Weltwirtschaft, ein neues Verständnis der Geschlechter und natürlich um den Aufbruch zu einer neuen Kunst. Doch Hammershøi verweigert sich diesem Sog wie kein zweiter. Die Zeit rast, die Welt gerät aus den Fugen, doch Hammershøi verharrt. Geboren 1864 und gestorben 1916, deckt seine Lebensspanne die vielleicht radikalste Periode ab, die die Kunst der Neuzeit erlebt hat. Doch Hammershøi antwortete darauf mit einer radikalen Verweigerung: Wenn um ihn herum Tempo aufgenommen wird, drückt er auf die Bremse, wenn der Farbrausch der Expressionisten auf der Leinwand beginnt, dann malt er weiter in Weiss und Grau, und wenn die Natur erobert wird, dann bleibt er zu Hause. Hammershøi malt weiter seine Innenräume aus und in Kopenhagen, ganz gleich, ob sich um ihn herum der Symbolismus, der Neo-Impressionismus, der Jugendstil, der Expressionismus, der Kubismus oder der Futurismus als Ausdruck seiner Zeit etablieren. Hammershøi sieht das alles, aber er sieht eben auch, dass sein Weg ein anderer ist. Diese Widerstandskraft, diese singuläre Resilienz gegenüber dem Lauf der Zeit schenkt seinen Bildern ihre innere Kraft.

Das Ausserordentliche dieses Malers erschliesst sich erst mit unserem heutigen Blick auf die Kunstgeschichte nach seinem Tod. Er nahm die Atmosphäre der rätselhaften Interieurs von René Magritte genauso vorweg wie die gemeisselten Rückenansichten Oskar Schlemmers. Auch die Magie der Verlorenheit auf den Bildern von Andrew Wyeth oder Edward Hopper scheint sich aus Hammershøis Werken abzuleiten, auch wenn sie ihn alle kaum kennen konnten. Das Unscharfe, das nur noch Erinnerte sowie der bewusste Verzicht auf bunte Farbigkeit finden schliesslich in den abgemalten Fotografien Gerhard Richters eine adäquate Fortsetzung.

So hielt also Hammershøi in seiner Kunst die Zeit an, bis in dem langen Jahrhundert danach die Zeit eine neue Kunst erschuf, die er schon längst zuvor geträumt hatte. Ja, Hammershøi erahnte unsere Sehnsüchte, lange bevor sie entstanden sind. Gerade, weil seine Bilder, Bilder über das Verbergen sind, also zeitlose Erzählungen über das Unsagbare, sagen sie uns so viel in unserer geheimnislosen Zeit.

•

Zeitgenossenschaft. Eigentlich bedeutet Zeitgenossenschaft, dass es einen geteilten Erfahrungsraum gibt, ein gemeinsames Erleben und ein gemeinsames Lebensgefühl. Sie beschreibt eine Verwandtschaft innerhalb einer synchronen Zeit. Hammershøis Bilder zeigen jedoch: Vielleicht lassen sich gemeinsame, geteilte Erfahrungen auch als ein Lebensgefühl über die Zeiten hinweg erzählen. Als ein Erahnen und Erinnern, das von einem Wissen eigentlich nicht mehr zu unterscheiden ist.

Kein Künstler dringt aus eigener Kraft aus den Tiefen der Verdrängung an die Oberfläche einer anderen Zeit, eines anderen Jahrhunderts: Das Wiederentdecken ist kein Zufall, sondern eine bewusste Handlung aus der jeweiligen Gegenwart heraus. Wir entdecken also nur wieder, was unsere aktuellen Bedürfnisse erfüllt; das, worin wir unser Heute und unsere Sehnsüchte wiedererkennen; das, worin unsere Zeit schon enthalten ist. Wir projizieren durch das Wiederentdecken die Vergangenheit auf unsere Gegenwart. Das Präsens, in dem Hammershøi seine grossen Fragen so still wie beharrlich an seine Zeit stellt – die Frage nach dem Geheimnis hinter allem, die Frage nach der Stellung der Frau, dem Überleben der Menschheit, dem Zwischenreich zwischen Traum und Wirklichkeit und dem Sog der Melancholie der Innerlichkeit –, das ist die in seine Vergangenheit eingeschriebene Gegenwart. Gegenwart, die mit unserem heutigen Betrachten sofort wieder aktiviert und von Neuem zum Jetzt werden kann.

•

Vermeers Luft. Hammershøis grosses Vorbild war Jan Vermeer, vor allem das Bild *Brieflesendes Mädchen am offenen Fenster* (Abb. 1, S. 31). Die angehaltene Luft von Vermeers Interieurs, die aufgeladene Atmosphäre der Räume, diese stille Energie der Delfter Malerei des 17. Jahrhunderts, das war genau die geheimnisvolle Aura, die Hammershøi in seine Gegenwart transportieren wollte.

Es gibt eine laute Geschichte der Kunst, also Künstler, die mit ihren Farben und Gesten und Kompositionen auf die Pauke hauen – Peter Paul Rubens etwa, Caravaggio, Francisco de Goya, Eugène Delacroix, Pablo Picasso. Das hat Hammershøi nicht interessiert. Er steht in der langen Reihe der stillen Geschichte der Kunst, die bei Cimabue begonnen hat, der italienischen Malerei des Quattrocento, Piero della Francesca vor allem. Die sich bei Chardin fortsetzte, bei Pieter de Hooch und bei Vermeer besonders, und die dann von Hammershøi aus weitergehen wird zu den intensiven und doch zurückhaltenden Gefügen Piet Mondrians und Giorgio Morandis. Was kann man wissen? Was kann man sehen? Kann Malerei mehr sein als die Verbreitung einer visuellen Information? Das sind die grossen Fragen dieser stillen Malerei – und Hammershøi stellt sie in jedem seiner Bilder aufs Neue.

Aber anders als Vermeer, bei dem die vereinzelten Gestalten durch subtile metaphorische und symbolische Anspielungen im Interieur aufgeladen und herausgefordert werden, steckt Hammershøi sie in Ausnüchterungszellen. Als sollten sie auch noch ihre letzten Emotionen und Zeitbezüge verlieren, versetzt Hammershøi seine Figuren in eine Art Hypnose, eine Trance. Und irgendwann beginnen scheinbar nicht nur die Gedanken seiner Figuren, sondern auch die Möbel und Räume selbst sich in einen Zustand der Ungreifbarkeit zu verwandeln. In einen Traum.

In der Strandgade 30 in Kopenhagen, in die er 1898 mit seiner Frau Ida einzog, baute er sich ein Heim der Zeitlosigkeit. Er widersetzte sich dem vollgestopften Zeitgeschmack der braunen Holzvertäfelung und schweren Möblierung und baute sich Stuben des holländischen 17. Jahrhunderts nach. Er liess alles hell und grau streichen und wählte Möbel aus der Zeit des Biedermeiers, die gerade aus der Mode gekommen waren. Er baute sich eine vollkommen abgeschlossene Raumkapsel inmitten einer vorwärtsstürmenden Moderne. Hammershøis Kunst war wie die Vermeers zu seiner Zeit auf eine geradezu aggressive Weise regressiv. Genau deshalb erscheint sie uns nun auf eine so subtile Weise progressiv.

Hammershøis Leben war so still wie seine Kunst. Er studierte, heiratete und zog in eine Wohnung. Die malte er. Dann zog er in eine andere Wohnung. Die malte er auch. Er hatte keine Kinder, er kämpfte in keinem Krieg. Er sass oft stundenlang in seinem Stuhl und blickte auf die Wand. Er kannte jedes Details der Kommode und des Klaviers. Jeden Luftzug. Manchmal ging er auf Reisen – viel häufiger, als man zunächst denkt: Er war in Paris, in London, in Berlin, in Rom. Aber all das, was er dort sah und erlebte, scheint er von sich zu weisen und mit einer entschiedenen Geste aussen vor zu lassen, wenn er vor der Staffelei in der Strandgade 30 sitzt, wenn er in sich hineinschaut. Daraus erzeugt er in seiner Kunst eine Atmosphäre maximaler Verdichtung. Konzentration. Stille. Hammershøi lädt seine Interieurs auf mit all dem, was er weglässt: Sie sind Widerstandsakte gegen die Zudringlichkeiten der Welt. Diese Kraft haben sie bis heute behalten.

In den Bildern von Hammershøi steht die Zeit und die Luft. Die Welt hält kurz ihren Atem an – und auch die Figuren verstummen, die in diesen Bildern stehen oder durch sie wandeln, seine Frau Ida vor allem. Es fällt kein Wort. Stattdessen: Andacht, Wundern, Ergriffensein. Es dauert nicht lange und Hammershøis Stille legt sich auch über unsere unruhigen Augen. Und wir lassen uns betören von der unendlichen Sehnsucht und Wehmut, die wie ein eigenartiges Licht aus allen Dämmerungen seiner Bilder herausstrahlt.

•

Gespenster. Hammershøi verwandelt die Menschen in seinen Werken in scheue Gespenster. Seine Interieurs wirken wie die Bühnenbilder für die Theaterstücke seiner skandinavischen Zeitgenossen Henrik Ibsen und August Strindberg, diffuse Beschwörungen der Abwesenheit.

In Strindbergs *Gespenstersonate* aus dem Jahre 1908 findet sich eine Gesellschaft in einem feierlichen Esszimmer ein. Die Figuren sind in diesem Raum und in ihren erfundenen Geschichten gefangen – sie finden keinen Weg heraus, zurück ins Leben. In Ibsens *Gespenster* (1881) geht es um die Erinnerung, die die Gegenwart überschattet und dazu führt, dass «wir allesamt Gespenster sind», wie es da heisst. Es gehe nicht nur um das, was in den Menschen herumgeistere an alten Gedanken, auch die Räume seien voll davon, überall würden «Gespenster herumschleichen»: Menschen, Gefühle, Bedrohungen. «Darum sind wir auch alle so gotterbärmlich lichtscheu, wir alle miteinander.» Da ist die Angst der eingeschlossenen Gestalten Strindbergs. Das ist die Angst der eingeschlossenen Gestalten Hammershøis. Sie sind so lichtscheu, weil sie zu Menschen werden müssten, wenn sie ihre schummrigen Wohnungen verlassen könnten. Genau das macht Hammershøis Werke so unheimlich und so modern in ihrer Angst: Man will die Klinken seiner weissen Türen niederdrücken und dahinter schauen, man weiss nur nicht, was dahinter liegt, das Paradies oder die Hölle.

•

Die Rolle der Frau. Die Gestalten bei Hammershøi sind fast immer weiblich und fast immer ist ein und dieselbe Frau sein Modell: Ida, seine Gattin, die er früh heiratete und die er in unzähligen Gemälden von hinten in ihrer gemeinsamen Wohnung porträtierte. Sie trägt den Idealkörper des Quattrocento wie einen Schleier um sich und erinnert an die feierlichen Figuren eines Masolino oder Perugino.

Aber natürlich sind es auch Vermeers Frauen und vor allem Caspar David Friedrichs Bild seiner Ehefrau Caroline, die berühmte, ebenfalls von hinten gemalte *Frau am Fenster* (1822), die Hammershøi früh kennenlernte und lebenslang prägen wird (Abb. 2, S. 35). Immer wieder sehen wir Ida in den Bildern: Sie steht versonnen mit einer Schüssel unter dem Arm, sie liest eine Zeitung, sie steht vor einem Klavier. Sie traumwandelt durch die Räume der gemeinsamen Wohnung. Ist sie verloren? Ist sie versonnen? Ist sie glücklich? Ist sie lebensmüde? Wir wissen es nicht.

Alle Gemälde Idas wirken wie Standbilder aus einem unendlichen Film ohne Handlung. Sie erinnern darin an eine der berühmtesten Fotoserien der jüngeren Kunstgeschichte, an die *Untitled Film Stills* von Cindy Sherman, die etwa hundert Jahre nach Hammershøis ersten Gemälden entstanden sind, in der Zeit zwischen 1977 und 1980 (Abb. 3, S. 36). In den Fotos sind scheinbare Standbilder aus einem

Film der Vergangenheit zu sehen, in denen die weibliche Hauptfigur, die immer Sherman selbst ist, in unterschiedliche Posen und Rollen schlüpft, deren Narrativ sich aber nicht auflösen lässt und das nur durch uns, in der Betrachtung vollendet werden kann. Shermans Ziel war es, nahezu ausdruckslose Bilder, kurz vor der Fiktion, zu kreieren. Zugleich spielt sie mit den kollektiven Formen von Weiblichkeit und Häuslichkeit. Hammershøi liess seine Frau Ida hundert Jahre zuvor ein ähnliches Spiel mit der weiblichen Identität aufführen – und doch liess er sie eigentlich nur die Rolle spielen, die sie ohnehin ausübte. Interessant ist dabei, dass Sherman ihre Figuren (also sich selbst) in Interieurs aus den 1940er-Jahren zurückversetzt, um alte Rollenklischees zu nutzen, und Hammershøi durch das Biedermeier-Mobiliar sowie die schlichte Kleidung seine Frau in die Welt der 1840er-Jahre zurückwirft. In beiden Fällen wird nichts erklärt, nichts erzählt, alles ist opak.

Wenn Hammershøis Frau ans Klavier tritt, dann spielt sie nicht, wenn sie an einem Tisch steht, dann berührt sie nicht ihre Tasse. Es gibt keine Handlung. Es gibt nur die Möglichkeit einer Handlung. Es lässt sich ahnen, dass in ihren Gedanken die Möglichkeit langsam zu einer Unmöglichkeit wird.

Dieses Sichtbarmachen der seelischen Innenwelt verbindet Hoppers Gemälde mit denen von Hammershøi. Auch Hopper hatte nur ein einziges Modell, seine Ehefrau Josephine, auch hier ist es ein jahrzehntelanges Kreisen eines Paares um sich selbst, das zu einer Malerei führt, bei der die Intimität immer wieder in Klaustrophobie umzuschlagen droht.

Denn auch bei Hopper gibt es eine grosse Vorliebe für den Innenraum und den Schutz vor den Bedrohungen der Aussenwelt, den er der dargestellten Ehefrau bietet. Nur das Licht darf in diese abgeschottete Welt hineinfallen (Abb. 4, S. 39). Hoppers Frau sitzt auf dem Bett, auf dem Sofa, an der Bar, die Welt ist moderner geworden, doch die Gedanken nicht. Wer bin ich? Was ist meine Rolle in dieser Welt? Warum sollte ich je wieder vor die Tür gehen? Ist Isolation nicht auch eine Rettung?

Die tiefe Melancholie dieser ewigen Fragen weht vom alten Europa Hammershøis direkt hinüber in die Neue Welt Hoppers.

•

Wiederholungszwänge. Zu Lebzeiten von Hammershøi entwickelte Sigmund Freud den Begriff des Wiederholungszwangs. Dieser beschreibt den manischen Impuls, auch schmerzhafte Träume oder Handlungen zu wiederholen. Hammershøis Wiederholungszwang bestand darin, seine Wohnungen in der Strandgade anzustarren und immer wieder aufs Neue zu malen. Genau das ist zentral für die Modernität seines Werkes, denn dieses Zwanghafte unterläuft aufs Überzeugendste die scheinbare Harmlosigkeit seiner Werke.

Es ist wie bei einem Fotografen, der immer dasselbe Motiv fotografiert oder wie bei einem Musiker, der immer denselben Ton spielt – auf diese besessene Weise widmet sich Hammershøi seiner Wohnung. Immer wieder sorgt er für geringe Veränderungen, stellt ein Möbelstück zur Seite oder holt einen Stuhl hinzu, schliesst eine Tür oder öffnet eine andere. Aber gerade in diesen kleinen Varianten entpuppt sich die Modernität des Serienhaften, die Monet mit seinen Heuschobern begonnen hat. Es ist immer wieder Ida, die Hammershøi wie in einem Puppenhaus in einen anderen Raum stellt und die er mit immer neuen Accessoires aus der kleinen Menge an Hausrat in Verbindung bringt. Das ist deshalb so neu, weil den Bildern das Ereignishafte völlig fehlt; es ist die Abwesenheit dessen, die sie so aufregend macht.

Hammershøi scheint die ganze Welt in seinen Räumen aufgehoben zu haben. Wie in Gefässen sind in seinen Bildern die Wünsche und die Ängste seiner Frau und seiner Zeit gestaut. Genau diese Verdichtung der Atmosphäre und des Motivischen, macht die Verbindung seiner Malerei mit den Stillleben Morandis so plausibel. Der italienische Maler bildete in seinem abgeschotteten Atelier die Vielfalt der Welt und ihre Achsenverschiebungen allein mit dem Neuarrangement von Flaschen und Krügen auf seinem Tisch ab (Abb. 5, S. 41). In der scheinbaren Ereignislosigkeit wird die kleinste Nuance zur Sensation und die gedeckte Farbpalette in ihrer Monotonie erinnert an die Reduktion der Farbigkeit bei Hammershøi. Auch wenn diese bei Morandi eher ins Gelbliche und Rötliche tendiert, während sie bei Hammershøi höchstens einmal ins Bräunliche abgleitet in dem dumpfen Zwielicht des Innenraums, das die Bilder beider Künstler verbindet. Hammershøi malt die Tür und das Piano so ernsthaft und aufmerksam, als seien sie Menschen, genau so wie Morandi dies mit dem Krug und der Flasche vollbringt: Die reduzierte Dingwelt wird für die, die schauen können, zu einem unendlichen Universum.

Die fahlen, in der Wiedergabe eines Moments eingefrorenen Bilder Morandis und Hammershøis fordern das Auge dennoch heraus. Man sucht nach den Nuancen und den Abweichungen. Die obsessive Wiederkehr eines Motivs, die sich mit der kaum spürbaren Modulation des Lichts verbündet, verschleiert so den eigentlichen Inhalt. Es ist eine völlige Absage an die klassische Erzählstruktur. Genau deshalb kann die Bildstruktur bei Hammershøi, also der Raum und der Mensch darin, als die ewiggültige Ideologie der Malerei hervortreten. So wie es der deutsche Dichter Rainer Maria Rilke beschrieb, als er Hammershøi und seine Kunst persönlich kennengelernt hatte: «Sein Werk ist lang und langsam und in welchem Augenblick man es auch erfassen mag, es wird immer voller Anlass sein, vom Wichtigen und Wesentlichen in der Kunst zu sprechen.»

•

Austernschalen. Die dezente Palette Hammershøis passt sich seiner dezenten Umgebung an: die weissen Türen und Fenster, die grauen Wände und Decken, das warme Honigbraun der Biedermeier- und Empiremöbel. Das sind seine Farben, mehr braucht er nicht. Wenn er raus blickt auf die Stadt, dann braucht er nur das Grau und die Milchigkeit eines getupften Weiss. Ein herrliches Silbergrau und darüber immer wieder die zarten Töne wie pulvriger Schnee. Und wenn er hinausgeht in die Natur, dann kommt ein verschwommenes, fahles Grün hinzu, wie kurz vorm Verdämmern. Das ist alles.

Eigentlich ist Hammershøis Farbwelt aber ein Universum in Grau. Als der dänische Maler Joakim Skovgaard einmal einen Blick auf Hammershøis Palette werfen durfte, war er hingerissen von dessen Limitationen. Er sprach von vier weißen und grauen Farben, die so genau miteinander vermalt waren, «als lägen vier Austernschalen auf seiner Palette.» Aus diesen Austernschalen entwarf Hammershøi dann die Perlen seiner Kunst.

Die pudrig getupfte Farbe auf seinen Leinwänden wird rhythmisiert durch das Licht. Es ist der geheime Regisseur jedes seiner Bilder. Dieses irritierend diffuse Licht, das die Räume seiner Wohnung durch eine unterschiedliche Tageszeit, einen anderen Einfallswinkel oder eine verschattende Wolke immer in neue Bilder verwandeln konnte.

Gerade dieses Spiel mit der verwandelnden Kraft des Lichts strahlt auch hinüber in die amerikanische Moderne, zu Hopper, aber eben auch zu Andrew Wyeth (Abb. 6, S. 42). «Ist da eigentlich», so fragte die New York Times schon 1998 in völliger Überraschung, «irgendein Unterschied zwischen Hammershøis dänischen Wohnungen und den weißen Häusern von Wyeth, erhellt vom fahlen Winterlicht? Beide Künstler haben einen melancholischen Sinn für das Ephemere und einen Naturalismus der Nostalgie.»

Dieser besondere Umgang mit dem Licht und das subtile Spiel mit Schwarz und Weiss verbindet Hammershøi auch mit den grossen fotografischen Lichtkünstlern seiner Zeit, mit Alfred Stieglitz und Heinrich Kühn etwa. Er entmaterialisiert die Welt durch die Körnigkeit seiner Malerei, und sie erinnert in ihrer reduzierten Farbigkeit und Standbildhaftigkeit immer wieder an die frühe Fotografie. Hammershøi hat wohl immer wieder Fotografien als Grundlage für seine Bilder genommen, er wusste um deren besondere Qualitäten in der Reduktion der Tonigkeit und kompositorischen Klärung. Dies führt direkt zu dem Verschmelzen der Dinge in den gemalten Fotografien Richters in den 1960er-Jahren: Das Ungreifbare, das dort zum Thema wird, die Lust an der Unschärfe und vor allem der stille Zweifel am Medium Fotografie deckt sich mit Hammershøis stillem Zweifel am Medium Malerei (Abb. 7, S. 45).

•

Nach dem Ball. Die so lockende wie schmerzhafte Stille, die über jeder einzelnen Leinwand Hammershøis liegt, speist sich aus einer leisen Trauer. Es sind alles Bilder des Abschieds. Hammershøi scheint sich bereits aus dem 20. Jahrhundert zurückzuziehen, obwohl es eigentlich noch gar nicht begonnen hat. Auch an seine Frau Ida scheint er sich nur noch wie an einen Traum zu erinnern, der langsam, je mehr man die Augen öffnet, immer ungreifbarer wird. Die Zimmer seiner Wohnung in Kopenhagen, das Mobiliar, jedes Bild wirkt wie ein letzter Blick zurück. Die ausgeblutete Grisaille seiner Palette verstärkt diesen Effekt.

Ein letzter Blick zurück. Nur auf was? Die Räume sind schon fast leergeräumt und nahezu unbelebt. Auch die wenigen Landschaften und Gehöfte wirken verlassen, da fliegt kein Vogel mehr und es weht kein Wind und in den kahlen Strassen und ausgezehrten Häusern, die er von aussen malt, scheint kein Mensch überlebt zu haben. Alle sind von uns gegangen.

Es scheint, als wolle Hammershøi in jenem Moment der Weltgeschichte, als die Beschleunigung ihre ungeheure Dynamik entfaltet, bereits eine Welt malen, aus der die Zentrifugalkräfte die Menschen hinausgeschleudert haben. Nur Ida scheint noch geblieben: ein letzter Mensch, den er malt bei ihrem letzten Kontrollgang durch die leergefegten Räume, bevor auch sie gehen muss, auf leisen Sohlen, um die finale Stille nicht zu stören, die sich schon über alles gelegt hat.

Die *Innenansicht der Großen Halle in Lindegaarden* (1909, S. 72–73) vielleicht Hammershøis kühnstes Bild, erzählt von diesem Abschied. Es ist ein leerer Raum, nur die Ornamente an der Decke und an den Wänden erinnern noch daran, dass hier einmal das Leben tobte. Der Ballsaal erzählt bereits von einer Welt nach den Menschen, nach der letzten Generation, also vom Ende des Anthropozäns.

Hammershøis Bilder wirken, als sei die Welt an ihr Ziel gekommen. Als könne sie endlich wieder ganz bei sich sein. So bannt Vilhelm Hammershøi in jedem seiner Gemälde den kostbaren Moment auf die Leinwand, in dem Zeit und Ewigkeit sich berühren.

Further Reading

Essay by Felix Krämer

Emil Nolde, *Das eigene Leben: Die Zeit der Jugend 1867–1902* [1931], 4th edition (Cologne: DuMont Schauberg, 1963), 225.

On Hammershøi's reticence, see Emil Hannover, *Erindringer fra barndom og ungdom* (Copenhagen: Forening for Boghaandvaerk, 1966), 72.

On Peder Severin Krøyer's statement, see Kristian Zahrtmann, "Om Vilhelm Hammershøi," in *Berlingske Tidende* (Copenhagen), February 14, 1916.

Interview with Hammershøi: C. C. Clausen, "Naar udstilling nærmer sig." (II. Vilhelm Hammershøi), *Hver 8. Dag* (Copenhagen), 1907, 437ff.

On Hammershøi and Symbolismus, see Felix Krämer, "Vilhelm Hammershøi," in *Vilhelm Hammershøi* (Hamburg: Hamburger Kunsthalle, 2003), 9–27, esp. 24–27.

Maurice Maeterlinck, "Silence" in *The Treasure of the Humble*, trans. Alfred Sutro (London: Ballantyne, 1905), 3–21.

Essay by Florian Illies

Rainer Maria Rilke, "Über Kunst" (1898), in Rainer Maria Rilke, *Sämtliche Werke*, vol. 5 (Frankfurt am Main: Insel-Verlag, 1965), 426–34, esp. 431–32.

Henrik Ibsen, Gengagere (1881), published in English as *Ghosts*, in *The Works of Henrik Ibsen*, trans. William Archer (New York: Charles Scribner's Sons, 1911), 280.

Sigmund Freud, *Erinnern, Wiederholen und Durcharbeiten (Weitere Ratschläge zur Technik der Psychoanalyse II)* (1914), in Freud, *Studienausgabe, Ergänzungsband* (Frankfurt am Main: Fischer, 2000), 205–15.

Rainer Maria Rilke, letter to Alfred Bramsen, dated November 10, 1905, quoted in Anne Hemkendreis, "The Essence of Things: Hammershøi as Seen through the Eyes of Rainer Maria Rilke," in *Hammershøi and Europe*, ed. Kasper Monrad (Copenhagen: Statens Museum for Kunst; Munich: Kunsthalle der Hypo-Kulturstiftung; Prestel, 2012), 179n1.

Joakim Skovgaard on Hammershøi's palette, quoted in *Politiken* (Copenhagen), February 14, 1916; reprinted in Poul Vad, *Vilhelm Hammershøi and Danish Art at the Turn of the Century*, trans. Kenneth Tindall (New Haven and London: Yale University Press, 1992), 364.

Holland Cotter, "A Dane Who Turned Nature and Copenhagen into Still Lives," *The New York Times*, July 3, 1998, section E, 31.

Photo Credits

bpk/Nationalgalerie, SMB/Jörg P. Anders: p. 35; bpk/Staatliche Kunstsammlungen Dresden/Wolfgang Kreische: p. 31; Collection of the Farnsworth Art Museum, Rockland, Maine, Museum purchase, 1964.1313: p. 42; Damian Griffiths: p. 61; Courtesy of Hauser & Wirth Collection Services: p. 41; Photo © The Hirschsprung Collection: p. 7; Galerie Knoell: pp. 49, 77–79; Det Kongelige Bibliotek, Copenhagen: pp. 11, 24–25; Antony Makinson of Prudence Cuming Associates, London: pp. 23, 55–57; Museum of Copenhagen, Photo: Fritz Theodor Benzen: p. 10; The National Museum of Western Art, Tokyo, Photo: NMWA/DNPartcom: p. 15; Nationalmuseum Stockholm, Photo: Cecilia Heisser: p. 9; Ordrupgaard, Copenhagen, Photo: Anders Sune Berg; p. 13; Copyright 2024 Phillips Auctioneers LLC. All Rights Reserved: pp. 50, 58, 69, 75, 81; Private collection: pp. 52–53, 82–83; © Gerhard Richter 2024 (0035): p. 45; © Cindy Sherman, Courtesy the artist and Hauser & Wirth, Photo: Hauser & Wirth: p. 36; Statens Museum for Kunst, Copenhagen: p. 18; Annik Wetter: cover, pp. 20, 62–63, 65–67, 71–74; Yale University Art Gallery, New Haven (CT), USA, Album/Scala, Florence: p. 39

Published on the occasion of the exhibition
Vilhelm Hammershøi: Silence
Curated by Felix Krämer
Hauser & Wirth Basel
June 1–July 13, 2024

Vilhelm Hammershøi: Silence

www.hauserwirth.com

Concept: Carlo Knoell
Editorial support: Max Steib

Publisher: Michaela Unterdörfer
Managing editor: Mélanie Letoré
Project assistance: Nicole Keller
Copyediting and proofreading: Luise Pilz (German); Tas Skorupa (English)
Translation into English: Elizabeth Tucker

Book design: Kobi Benezri
Prepress: prints professional, Berlin
Production coordination: Christine Stricker
Printing and binding: DZA Druckerei zu Altenburg GmbH

Cover Paper: Pergraphica Natural smooth, 200 gsm
Paper: Pergraphica Natural smooth, 120 gsm
Typeface: Le Monde Livre Classic, ITC Bookman

Cover:
Vilhelm Hammershøi, *Interior with the Artist's Wife, Seen from Behind* (detail), 1901 (see p. 71)

ISBN: 978-3-906915-96-8

Library of Congress Control Number: 2024935699

Printed and bound in Germany

Distribution:
Europe and the UK
Buchhandlung Walther König
Ehrenstrasse 4
50672 Cologne

All other territories
ARTBOOK | D.A.P.
75 Broad Street, Suite 630
New York, NY 10004